S0-ABO-836

MAN AGAINST WOMAN

What Every Woman Should Know About Violent Men

Dr. Edward W. Gondolf

Western Psychiatric Institute and Clinic
University of Pittsburgh

Human Services Institute
Bradenton, FL

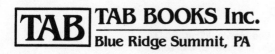

TAB BOOKS Inc.
Blue Ridge Summit, PA

FIRST EDITION
FIRST PRINTING, 1989

Library of Congress Cataloging in Publication Data

Gondolf, Edward W., 1948-
    Man against woman.

    Bibliography: p.
    1. Wife abuse—United States.   2. Conjugal violence—
United States.   3. Abused wives—United States—
Psychology.   I. Title.
HV6626.G64   1989   362.8'3   88-12992
ISBN 0-8306-9002-6 (p)

TAB BOOKS Inc. offers software for sale. For information and
a catalog, please contact TAB Software Department, Blue Ridge
Summit, PA 17294-0850.

Questions regarding the content of this book should be addressed to:

Human Services Institute, Inc.
P.O. Box 14610
Bradenton, FL 34280

Development Editor: Lee Marvin Joiner, Ph.D.
Design and Production: Margaret E. Dickson

Table of Contents

Foreword

Man Against Woman gives you information to better understand your partner's behavior. But first, we would like to give you some information to better understand yourself. We speak to you as two women who have worked with battered women for well over a decade. As workers in shelters for battered women, we have talked with thousands of women over the years. And we have found a few things that can turn a desire to "understand" a violent man into a misunderstanding of a dangerous situation and how to change it.

We know you may sincerely want to help your abusive or violent partner, and you may even feel responsible for fixing his violence. Our role as women has historically been to nurture and to support our loved ones *under any circumstances.* Unfortunately, we feel an obligation to "stand by our man" no matter what the cost to ourselves.

We, of course, should have some knowledge of a man's problems, but it can be dangerous to use that knowledge to excuse his behavior. If we are too concerned about "understanding" him, we may become too compassionate and forgiving of a man's abuse or violence. We may minimize the danger to ourselves and our children and undercut the responsibility a man must take for his own behavior.

We women also tend to get trapped into thinking that we are the only ones who truly understand our male partners. For example, we may know that our partner was abused as a child, saw his mother battered by his father, or was the child of an alcoholic parent. We are likely to feel sorry for him, and think that he can't help the way he is.

Consequently, we suffer tremendous guilt at the thought of leaving someone in so much "pain," especially if he is remorseful after the violence and is convincing in his stated desire to change. How can we leave a man like this when we're sure no one will understand him the way we do? The reality is that your love for him alone will not make him change.

The best thing you can do for a violent man is to take care of yourself. You have to set some clear limits. Often, this means leaving a partner. This not only provides safety for you, but also will impress upon your partner the seriousness of his behavior. Contacting a shelter for battered women is one way of seeking safety. Shelters can also be a source of strength in determining your options. Most shelters can help with resources, legal information, parenting, and overall support. But the primary concern of most shelters is for *your* safety and not *his* well-being.

You may not always want to hear what shelter staff say is best for you. Even if you do not agree with what you may hear, please accept that all shelters want to help you and keep you safe. The staff share the experience of many women like yourself. They, along with countless other women in your community, created the shelters for women like you, and they will always be there for you when you are ready to make some changes in your life. Even if you do not actually choose to stay in a shelter, all shelters have a crisis line you can call. (See the appendix on "Hotlines" for how to obtain your local shelter phone number or other referral assistance.)

Whether you contact a shelter or not, it is important to understand that your partner's violence is not your fault and you cannot change him. Ultimately, you will have to take responsibility for your own life, even if you believe it will hurt him. Whatever actions he takes after you leave are his choice. As this book suggests, there are several options he may consider.

We think *Man Against Woman* also sends this message. It should arm you with facts that will keep you from falling into the traps we've outlined here. The book is based on the counseling and research experience of a person who has worked with violent men for several years. We first met the author of *Man Against Woman*, Edward W. Gondolf, over four years ago at the Third International Institute on Victimology. Since then we have invited him to participate in our own training conferences and have followed his many writings on violent men. In fact, Dr. Gondolf and one of us (Ellen R. Fisher) recently published a book entitled *Battered Women as Survivors*, which is a study based on interviews with thousands of women in Texas shelters. All this is a way of saying that Dr. Gondolf stands as one of the experts in the field who we respect very much.

It is essential that you begin to see yourself as an expert too. As Dr. Gondolf also insists, you know your situation better than anyone. We are simply urging you to look at it honestly. Trust your instincts over your doubts and hesitations. Don't just try to cope, appease, or outmaneuver your partner. Do something to assure your safety. There are many of us who would like to help you in this endeavor. There are many women like you who have made changes in their lives. Reading a book like this should help make such a change in your life, too--- one that includes an end to violence.

Ellen R. Fisher
Executive Director
La Casa de las Madres
San Francisco, CA

Judy Reeves
Shelter Outreach Director
Center for Battered Women
Austin, TX

July 26, 1988

Introduction

If you seek some realistic answers to questions about violent men, then this book is for *you*, whether you are an abused woman or someone who helps them. Why is he so violent toward me? Will he ever change? Do men's counseling programs really work? Abused women ask these questions again and again about their batterers. They ask out of a desire for safety and change.

Man Against Woman offers an in-depth look at violent men that is free of blanket stereotypes or simplistic solutions. It presents a readable digest of the latest clinical observations and research findings. It also draws on the author's extensive experience as a man working with programs for men who batter women.

Man Against Woman is not, however, just another advice book outlining how women ought to think and act. The idea of this book is to give women the essential information, so they can make their own decisions about their unique situation. The reasons for the violence and the chances for nonviolence are discussed.

What's not considered are the many emotional tugs, financial pressures, self-doubts, and deep fears that affect a woman's thinking about her abusive relationship. Each woman must address these *herself*, with support or counsel from other women or women's shelter staff. Moreover, several excellent guidebooks written by women for battered women are already available to aid in this effort. Many of these are listed in the *Resources* section of this book.

Man Against Woman answers the most frequently asked questions about violent men. **Part One** of *Man Against Woman* reveals the reasons for men's violence towards women, and how it occurs. **Part Two** considers whether violent men can and will change. Using these insights, the reader should have a more accurate picture of the partner's actions and motives. And the book should help answer the crucial question, "What should I do now?"

The reasons men are violent toward women are complex, but still clear. *Man Against Woman*, as the title suggests, sees this violence as part of a tendency in our society to devalue, subject, and control women. Much of what a battered woman experiences is an extension of this tendency. There are individual circumstances that add to this tendency, things like alcohol abuse. But the result is a distorted sense of masculinity that drives many men to be violent, abusive and controlling of women---a system of beliefs that pits man against woman.

Some say that a woman contributes to abuse. Many women feel, deep down inside, that battering was partly their fault. I disagree strongly. From my own work with batterers one thing is clear: Men must accept responsibility for their violence. A decisive truth about men is that they don't even begin to change until they put all the excuses for their abuse aside and face up to it. No woman made them abusive or violent. Neither did alcohol, a bad childhood, a hard day at work, oppression as a minority man, or "nagging" or arguing. Also, anger or a wicked temper don't make a man violent.

There are different types of violent men, each with different prospects for change and needs for different types of help. As you might hope, some men do stop their violence. Some stop their violence but continue to be emotionally or verbally abusive. A few men change *dramatically*, in every way including lifestyle.

Even if men do make an effort to change, however, it doesn't mean that they are "cured." Often they will tell you that they are "cured" after a few counseling sessions or a few weeks without violence. The reality is that change takes a long time---months and years, not hours and days. Change, to be permanent, must stem from an honest desire to be a different person, not simply to "get her back," or because of a court sentence. Many women may be unwilling to wait this long.

Women too are involved in the man's change process, *like it or not*. This doesn't mean, however, that they are responsible for their husband's or lover's change. A battered woman doesn't make her batterer change, just like she doesn't make him violent. What it does mean is that a woman's actions may reinforce some of her husband's or lover's efforts to stop being violent. For instance, a woman's leaving a violent man for her own safety may prompt him to seek help.

What may seem to be contradictions, are actually competing priorities. For example, there are some clear social and psychological reasons behind violence. But men must ultimately take responsibility for their own behavior and be motivated to change, despite these circumstances. To paraphrase Jesse Jackson, "You may be born in the slums, but the slums aren't born in you." Also, while it is useful for a battered woman to know more about violent men, knowing isn't the crucial priority. First, she must assure her own safety and take care of her own needs. She has to do what is right for her. And that is not to be found in him.

Throughout this book I refer to *violence* as any physical abuse of another person. Pushing, shoving, grabbing, slapping, punching, kicking, pulling hair, and choking are all forms of violence. Twisting an arm, holding a woman against her will, and forcing sex on her are also violent acts. Of course any use of a weapon, or throwing things at another person, is violence, too.

Abuse includes these violent acts plus the psychological, verbal, and financial ways someone can hurt another's self-esteem or potential. Control, coercion, intimidation, manipulation, and threats are all forms of abuse. *Battering* generally means the violent abuse of a woman.

Actual statements by violent men are used throughout the book to illustrate the main points. The quotations are from batterers who have been participating in batterer counseling programs for several months to several years. Many of the men are exceptional in that they have been free of violence for a year or more. Most batterers do not manage this kind of change.

The quotations offer important insights into the men's violence and the steps necessary for change. Some of the quotations in the book, and *A Man's Story* (Chapter 10), are composites of more than one man's comments. They illustrate a prevailing outlook or experience among the batterers we have encountered in our batterer program.

A more detailed look at how batterers see their own violence is presented in the following articles: "The Gender Warrior: Reformed Batterers on Abuse, Treatment, and Change," by Edward W. Gondolf and James Hanneken, in *Journal of Family Violence* 2:2 (1987): pp. 177-190; and "Why Do Men Batter Their Wives," by James Ptacek, in *Feminist Perspectives on Wife Abuse*, edited by K. Yllo and M. Bograd (Newbury Park, CA: Sage Publications, 1988). Additional case studies of batterers are found in *Man to Man: A Guide for Men in Abusive Relationships*, by Edward W. Gondolf and David M. Russell (Bradenton, FL: Human Services Institute, 1987) and *Men Who Batter: An Integrated Approach to Stopping Wife Abuse*, by Edward W. Gondolf (Holmes Beach, FL: Learning Publications, 1985). A bibliography of the research summarized in this book is available in *Research on Men Who Batter: An Overview, Bibliography and Resource Guide*, by Edward W. Gondolf (Bradenton, FL: Human Services Institute, 1988).

To my parents,

with appreciation for their

good example.

Part One

The Reasons

Chapter 1

Aren't All Men Violent?

There is ample evidence to answer this question with an emphatic "Yes." Men seem to have violence "in their blood." Not only do men eagerly march off to war, but they play at war through football, boxing, and other contact sports. Some psychologists go as far as saying that aggression, which all too often turns into violence, is a natural part of survival. Men must compete, conflict, and even fight to stay alive and, oddly enough, improve themselves. Psychologists add that women are as capable of this aggression and violence, even though our society tends to limit their expression of it.

This way of thinking can be a trap. While violence at times seem to be all around us, it doesn't have to be. It isn't inevitable and doesn't have to be tolerated. Moreover, the violence of men against women is more than a spillover from the unruly world around us. It is a symptom of a set of misguided beliefs called "the male sex role."

PRIVILEGE AND PATRIARCHY

Men are violent toward women for much more complex reasons than just acting out a violent nature.
The violence is more than just "boys being boys."
The violence is often the result of men acting out
their sense of privilege toward women. It is a way
to keep women, and also children, under control and
in their place. It is men trying to live up to the
male sex role.

The male sex role includes a rigid set of expectations about the rights and privilege of men and the
submissive role of women. These expectations are
apparent in this batterer's thoughts about why he
became violent:

*"I remember being at work and expecting to
come home and find the house clean, dinner on the
table, and my wife with her pants off waiting for
me. I'd get there and find just the opposite. The
house is a mess, and the last thing my wife wants
is to go to bed. I realize now that she couldn't
read my mind. I had all these expectations that
were bound to make me disappointed when I got
home."*

These expectations represent a sense of male
privilege. Most men are brought up thinking that
it's their right to be in charge, provide for women,
protect women, be served and cared for by women.
Women are too often objects for their pleasure and
use. Men feel like they're supposed to "wear the
pants" in the household. What they say goes.

4

Men learn from the time they are born that they are in charge of women. We learn this from the playground where we prove ourselves not "sissy" or "queer," in sports where female cheerleaders praise and encourage us, and from movies where invincible heroes like Superman and Rambo save those in distress. In fact, we often define our masculinity in terms of how powerful we are or feel we are.

The sense of power men crave is more than a leftover from growing up. It remains, despite the many changes in our society, a harsh reality of America. It is still "a man's world" when it comes to important decisions, high finance, and international affairs. This *patriarchy*, or male dominated world, extends into most households. Men think they should rule there as they do outside the home. "A man's home is his castle." As one man recalled the way he thought the home was supposed to be:

"My father ruled the house. His word was law. My mother would always say, 'You will have to wait until we talk to your father,' or if I did something wrong, 'Wait until your father comes home.' He did what he wanted. He would paint the house pink, if he felt like it, and you'd better like it or else...."

FEAR OF FEMININITY

Behind the facade of privilege and power is an insecurity that haunts many men. At the same time most men feel they have a right to get what they want from women, they also have a fear that at

5

any time they can easily be undone. This is especially evident in sexual relations, when intimacy is avoided through abuse or impotency. In the process of our being tough and competitive, we men learn to suppress our emotions. Emotions are something men don't deal with well, in themselves or others.

Women appear to us to be more expressive, more emotional and, at times, truly irrational. So we try to turn them off with abuse or by withdrawing entirely. As one woman batterer explains, "I resented her for being so open, when I had difficulty doing this..." Another man noted the male-female differences:

"Women can verbally abuse you. They can rip your clothes off, without even touching you, the way women know how to talk. But men don't know how to do this as well. They weren't brought up to talk as much as women do. So we resort to violence, if we can't get through to a woman by words."

Some psychologists suggest that the fear of femininity goes deeper, to an unconscious level. Men fear women's attachment to nature, as seen in the birthing process. It's a process that leaves us on the outside looking in. Moreover, femininity is linked to nurturing, tenderness, vulnerability, cooperation, and patience. To some men, these qualities amount to weakness and therefore make them feel uneasy. Men degrade, attack and abuse those perceived as weak as a means of asserting their own tenuous strength. By putting women down, they

6

lift themselves up to where they think they should be: *in charge*. According to one man:

> *"You just have to let a woman know who is in charge once in awhile. Otherwise, she'll walk all over you. You know they have this wild side that can play tricks on you. You have to keep a watch out or they'll take you over, and you'll be at their mercy."*

SEXUAL VIOLENCE

A devastating form of violence for a woman is marital or acquaintance rape. About one-third of battered women report experiencing sexual violence, and probably many more have been pressured into sex against their will. A recent nationwide survey of college students estimated that about one in five of the students had been raped or experienced attempted rape by an acquaintance. There is no doubt that for many men, sex and violence are closely linked. Again, the male sex role contributes to this association. Sex, like violence, for many men is a release of frustration and anger, and an assertion of power and privilege. Much of our locker room talk bears this out. Sex becomes a contest, like a sport. We brag and taunt one another about the women we've had. The pressure and expectations mount.

The beliefs of many men seem to fall into two categories. One is that they believe, in their ignorance of women, that women "really want it." They excuse their violence as something women like, even when

7

they say, "No". While men sometimes receive mixed signals from women, that's not really the problem. Men too often have a set interpretation and response before those signals are sent. The other belief is that there is a *deal* involved in male-female relationships. Whenever a man spends money on a women or shows her a good time, he deserves sex in return. This leaves many women trapped in a no win situation, especially since many don't have their own funds or feel pressure to go along with the man in order to be accepted. The situation is expressed by this man's feeling of his "rights":

"It is a belief of mine I guess. Women have this material thing. They are after a man's money. In return I expect something I want. If I show a woman a good time or spend a lot of money on her I expect something in return. And if I don't get it I take it. That something is sex."

Many battered women report that sex is used to lure them back into a relationship with a violent man, as well as a means to push them away. They say they mistake sex for love and acceptance, when it is often being used as a tool for manipulation. They want to feel close to someone and have their hurts eased. But what appears as pleasure turns too quickly into control and violence, especially given the violent man's fears of intimacy. To be too close is, for many men, to lose control and become vulnerable. These insecurities are evident in this man's comments:

"When we really have good sex — have it my way — I really feel good about myself. I really feel like a man. I've done what I'm supposed to do. But if it gets all mushy like and she starts making demands or complaining — well, then that's a different story. I mean a man needs a certain sense that he is in charge. You have to watch putting your guard down too much or you're likely to be blindsided — and, heaven forbid, by the woman you're married to.

CHILDREN AS VICTIMS

The violence too often spills over beyond the couple. Half of the children admitted to battered women's shelters have been abused or neglected. Almost a quarter of the mothers told of being abused while pregnant. The more severe the violence against the mother, the more likely there will be violence against the children. Threats against the children are used as the violence escalates. In many a woman's mind, potential harm of her children is the ultimate harm to her. The fear and desperation intensify, as it probably should. Not only are the children at risk of being physically harmed, they are likely to be emotionally scarred by the tension and violence between their parents. Ironically, it is the child abuse laws and fear for a child's safety that prompts many battered women to take action against their husbands or lovers.

Like the violence against women, violence against children can appear in several forms. As one batterer insisted in counseling:

9

"I don't know what happened. I guess I just snapped. I was playing pool with my 13 year old daughter and she broke one of the pool sticks. It was really an accident. And I hauled off and clobbered her a few times across the back with my stick. I really hurt her. She was black-and-blue the next day. I guess I wanted her to be more careful, but I just overreacted."

The violence here seems on the surface like a problem of impulse control. The man just lost his temper, or so he claims. But in a later comment by the same man, another side emerges.

"I've done a lot for all the kids. I mean I do love them to death. I've taken them to ball games, amusement parks, fishing and things like that. I like showing them a good time. But I deserve some respect and appreciation in return. When one of them pushes me aside to be with their stepdad or do such and such with their mother, I get mad. I have a responsibility to make them obey and I'll use punishment if I have to in order to get them to respond to me. That's all part of being a good father."

That need to control others, to be in charge, to fulfill one's sense of manhood, is revealed again. Men too often feel jealous that the mother is closer to the children than they are. They fight over whose word should be the last in disciplining them. Yet, too often they don't know how to be the nurturing fathers who would allow for genuine respect and closeness. They may even fear becoming a different kind of father. It means being something they don't know how to be and think they should not be – a caring, open, and vulnerable person.

TYPES OF BATTERERS

While all men have, to some extent, the same violent tendencies, there are also some obvious differences in what they do about them. Research studies have identified different types of men – what we call "the good, the bad, and the ugly." This classification does not mean that every man will neatly fit in one type or another. In fact, the types may form a continuum. A man might be on the borderline of two types or move from one type to another. For instance, it is common for some *sporadic batterers* to develop into *chronic batterers*. While all these men are potentially dangerous, those we call "the ugly guys" are obviously the most lethal – and the least likely to change.

Nonviolent Men – "The Good"

There are some "good guys" who are free of physical violence toward women. There is the *goody-goody* who speaks of treating women equally and doing his share of the housework. He claims he enjoys being with women and supports women's rights.

Even the *goody-goody* falls into mental abuse at times. He may control, pressure, or put down women, sometimes unintentionally, sometimes deliberately. These good guys, moreover, tend to feel that they are themselves put upon for going against

11

the patriarchy and being nice to women. They expect some reward for this.

Another kind of "good guy," at least to himself, is the more traditional *good old boy*, who sticks to the rules he puts down, sometimes rigidly. He is courteous and protective of women, as long as they treat him as a good guy. His remarks, however, are regularly colored with wisecracks about women. He tolerates women in positions of authority but doesn't prefer it. He'll slow things down by stonewalling to keep a "bitchy" woman in her place.

Women Batterers – "The Bad"

The "bad guys" are those who have physically abused (or battered) women, but have not been physically violent to non-family members. In fact, they may appear downright charming to those outside the family. They include sporadic batterers and chronic batterers. The *sporadic* batterers are those who tend to be passive or quiet and then, without much warning, explode. They tend to follow a violent incident with profuse apologies and promises not to do it again. This is commonly termed a *honeymoon period*. The tension slowly builds until he explodes again. This *cycle of violence* may be as short as a month or two or as long as six months to a year. These men are likely to feel some shame and seek help. However, they easily convince themselves during a honeymoon phase that the problem is past.

The *chronic* batterer is regularly abusive, verbally and physically. He is more likely to have abused the children and to have been sexually abusive. He is also more likely to have used a weapon, and is less likely to apologize for an incident. In fact, he will often blame and threaten the women after an incident. Or he might simply ignore and dismiss the abuse as "no big deal." Chronic batterers have little sense that they have done anything serious or wrong. It takes the police or a divorce to confront them with their abuse and move them toward considering change.

Generally Violent Men – "The Ugly"

The "ugly guys" are those men who are violent in and outside the home. They include both *antisocial* men and *sociopathic* men. *Antisocial* men cause severe injury and often "use" women. They are likely to have severe drug or alcohol problems and be in trouble with the law. Much of this behavior may be reinforced by a gang of other antisocial men. This type of batterer appears to have little regard for himself or others, and may even appear to have no self-control. His prospects of changing are therefore low, especially in short-term anger control counseling programs or individual therapy. He needs a combination of interventions and treatments lasting years.

Sociopathic men are generally antisocial but to an even greater extreme. They have long criminal records, severe alcohol *and* drug problems. Their destructive tendencies are an expression of a

13

sadistic attitude toward not only women but all other people. Their unruliness may appear to be a kind of raw power, but is probably linked to a severe mental disorder. These men usually need extensive psychiatric treatment in a supervised and restrictive setting.

NEW ROLES FOR MEN

There has been much speculation, or at least much hope, that men are changing. Several recent books, in fact, have described a "new man" emerging in the '80s. Books like *The New Male*, *A Choice of Heroes*, *How Men Feel*, and *Finding Our Fathers* all suggest that at least some men are becoming less violent and more accepting of feminine qualities. Much of this new view appears to be in response to the women's movement which has prompted men to take a harder look at themselves.

In the process, many men found the way they lived was not only harmful to women, but also had bad consequences for themselves. Much has been made of the short-life spans of men, shortened in part because of the reckless and stress-filled lives they tend to live. Some men have begun to realize that the male sex role has left them underdeveloped emotionally and out of touch with some of the joys of life. For instance, many men have failed to get to know their children or become truly close to other men.

While some changes appear to be under way, there has also been a tremendous backlash. Some men

14

have used this sense of "the new man" as a basis for further resentment against women. They claim women have failed to appreciate men's problems. Some argue that women now are getting all the breaks, and they fight for more "men's rights" in divorce settlements and custody cases. This outlook reflects the resentment raised by many batterers after they have been "caught." As one batterer in treatment notes after his second divorce:

"I mean it burns me. Look where I am now. I have had two houses and two marriages. It's probably cost me a hundred thousand dollars. And here I am with a car that doesn't work half of the time and sixteen dollars in my pocket. You know it's hard to let all that go by, I mean, just forget about it."

Most alarming is the increasing numbers of men who justify or excuse violence. While there are signs of an emerging "new male," the fascination with war, grizzly pornography, and "an eye-for-an-eye" philosophy are also growing. This trend may be a counter to the threat some men feel with all the changes going on around them. It is their way to reassert their lessening privilege and power. Comments from another man illustrate this trend:

"It may not have been right for me to hit her, but every one has some limits. She provokes it at times. I mean really asks for it by giving me such a hard time. I mean she doesn't let up. Just seeing how much she can get away with. It's all I can do to hold my own. The world and everything around

us is going to pot. A person has to take a stand once in a while and say, 'Enough is enough!'"

Summary

While most men are inclined to be violent, this is not an acceptable excuse for the abuse of women. The violence against women is tied to a sense of male privilege and power. It also stems from an underlying fear of the feminine. This is especially evident in the sexual abuse and child abuse that often accompany battering. Moreover, men do differ in how they fulfill the male sex role that represents these tendencies. There are different types of men; some who only psychologically abuse women, others who also physically batter women to varying degrees, and some who are violent to family members and unrelated people. Lastly, changes are taking place in American society that are making violence less acceptable to many men. Even though there is a frightening backlash to many of these changes, there is at least some sign that men not only should, but can be different. This is something women have a right to expect and encourage.

Chapter 2

Why Is He So Violent?

Many women are aware of the violent tendencies in society that reinforce or justify the abuse of women. But knowing this doesn't explain their own personal situation. As noted in the previous chapter, some men act less violently than others. Why then does a particular husband or lover act the way he does? Is there anything about his situation or his personality that makes him more violent than other men? The answers to these questions are often as varied as men themselves. But behind the varied answers are some common themes. These add up to an overreaction to the male sex role, something we call "the failed macho complex."

IS IT PSYCHOLOGICAL?

We commonly hear batterers described as having psychological problems. The implication is that they batter because of these psychological problems. They may have poor *impulse control*, low *tolerance to stress*, low *self-esteem* and poor *communication skills*. Some batterers may have also suffered *traumatic experiences* in the war. These problems may be made worse by alcohol or drug abuse. According to some psychologists, the psychological problems need to be treated in order to stop the violence.

Ironically, most batterers heartily deny that they are "crazy" in any way. A typical response is:

"I went to a couple of psychologists, but I knew I wasn't crazy. They were the one's that were off the wall. I mean they didn't understand what was going on with me at all."

Even though they deny that they are "crazy," men still plead psychological problems as an excuse for their violence, and thus perpetuate the violence that is supposedly being treated. As one batterer remarked:

"I got abusive because I lost control of my temper. I am just kind of impulsive, I guess. But I can't help it. That's just the way I am. In fact, I've always had trouble with my temper. I guess you'd say it's psychological or something."

While a violent husband or lover may have some psychological problems, so do many men who are not violent. In fact, some researchers would say men who are not violent toward women have many of the same psychological problems attributed to violent men. Studies using psychological tests have failed to show that batterers are that much different from other men. While psychological factors

18

may reinforce a tendency toward violence, they do not in themselves cause it.

PROBLEM FAMILIES

The shortcomings of psychological explanations have led some experts to look beyond the individual batterer to his family. They suggest that the "cause" of the abuse can be found in the family patterns of interaction: the expectations the man and woman have of each other, the way they communicate with each other, and the way they, as a couple, deal with the world around them. For instance, couples who share more of the household decisions are less likely to experience violence. Couples who argue a lot, according to the same study, are more like to escalate into violence. Moreover, there may be things that the woman does that contribute to the man's violence. In fact, she may be violent or aggressive herself. The implication here is that the husband and the wife have to be treated together.

This "problem family" view has been controversial. For one, it appears to imply that the woman has somehow helped cause or perpetuate the violence. Several studies have suggested, however, that most of the aggression from women is in self-defense or retaliation. As one man in a batterer program admits:

"Sometimes she gave it back to me as hard as I gave it to her. But yes, she was doing what I had taught her over years of punishment. Monkey-see-monkey-do, I guess. She was trying to fend me off

19

as best she knew how. She had gotten pretty desperate by then."

Also, accounts from battered women show that much of the male violence is unexpected and unprovoked. The man will "go off the handle" with little or no warning. As another man explains the pattern of his violence:

"I mean I would just haul off and hit her sometimes...without warning or anything. Wham! It would just happen. She would say something little or do something that normally didn't bother me. But at that time and place it triggered something. I can't really explain it. Like the other day I asked her to get me orange juice. She made some wise-crack about 'say please' and then brought me O.J. in a soapy glass. It irked me so I kicked the chair and threw a container of pencils at her."

Furthermore, most abusive families have turned into miniature "terrorist states" instead of "family systems" of interactions that can be neatly analyzed and treated. One batterer notes the state of his family:

"It had hit rock bottom. She was too scared to even look at me. I had done such damage to her emotionally and was so messed up myself that there was no way we could come together then. When we tried, it just caused more problems. I didn't realize it at the time, but we had to get away from each other for a while."

MULTIPLE CAUSES

An even more complicated explanation of violence is that multiple causes are involved. A combination of psychological, family, and social factors contribute to making someone violent; or as some social scientists prefer to say, *put a person at risk* of being violent. For instance, a man who has grown up in a violent family where there was little assertive communication, who abuses alcohol, is unemployed, has low income, and few friends will have a higher chance of becoming violent. These chances are increased when the community accepts male dominance and violence against women and doesn't provide resources for women and interventions to stop it. This is evident in this man's comments:

"I've gone through a lot, you know, and I'm sure that has affected my relationship. I've worked really hard to make some headway in my job, and then was laid off for a while. I mean you really have to compete hard or you can lose it all. Then you come home and are supposed to act real sweet and everything. There are just too many pulls in too many directions until you start to come apart."

This "multi-factor" view makes good sense on the surface. Violence is a complex matter. The more personal, family, and social problems, the more likely a man will react desperately *and* violently. The shortcoming here is that it is difficult to tell the forest for the trees. We are left feeling helpless and overwhelmed by all these complications. The view fails to show us where to start, to intervene, or what is at the root of it all.

THE FAILED MACHO COMPLEX

The challenge is to sort out the social factors and psychological contradictions into some meaningful order. The idea of the *failed macho complex* is one way to accomplish this. This idea suggests that a man becomes violent in an effort to live up to some distorted ideal of manhood. His abuse of women is a means of compensating for his feelings of inadequacy and a shortcut to being what he thinks he should be as a man.

Many batterers, at least on the surface, do not appear to live up to the "macho," power-hungry, male sex role described in Chapter One. Some psychological tests have, in fact, shown batterers to rate slightly lower on masculinity and self-esteem than other men. They seem to see themselves as falling short of the male sex role. As one man summarized his abusiveness:

"What angered me was myself. I wasn't content with who I was."

Another man concedes:

"I can't wallow in self-pity, I know. But basically I don't like myself too much."

As other research suggests, many batterers had little else but the society's male sex role to follow.

22

Their fathers were often abusive, leaving them with a poor role model and a sense they could never please him. This familiar theme is reflected in the recollections of this man:

"My father had been a drill sergeant who was hooked on discipline. We all grew up with 'what dad says goes.'"

Or, the men had distant fathers who left them to turn to the sex role images of the media or their peers to define themselves as a "man." One man expressed his mixed feelings toward his dad this way:

"My dad died of blood clots to the brain when I was young. It was of course a shock I'll never forget. He was a chain smoker who didn't eat right either. He complained of dizzy spells a lot... But he was basically a good man.... You know, I never talked back to him though. He had mean looks that scared me, it was just the intensity of the looks. But dad and I were good friends. He always came to my games. He was a good dad...but he was suddenly gone."

In many ways, the male sex role is impossible to fulfill and leaves men frustrated. According to one formerly violent man:

"Women don't realize the image us men get caught up in. We are supposed to be tough, don't show your feelings, and always in charge. You gotta bring home the bread and please everybody. Sure

23

you get some 'bennies' for it all, but it also has its toll. You get frustrated sometimes that you can't do it all. You can't be all that you're supposed to be."

Only a very few can be Rambo or "King of the Mountain." The rest are left fighting extra hard to be what we are not. The violence against women by many batterers may be, therefore, accomplishing two things. One, it is a way of taking out the frustration and self-hatred on women. Two, it is also a way of putting yourself "on top," so to speak. Abuse is a quick way for an insecure man to feel like a "man."

The *failed macho complex* has useful implications for dealing with batterers. They are:

1) Batterers need to have their violence decisively confronted by community authorities. This is a way of negating the male sex role they think is acceptable and necessary.

2) Men need to be educated about alternative images of manhood. They need to see the choices and opportunities they have to be different.

3) Batterers need reinforcement and support for their new self-image, and ways to counter the social pressures to be the "old man."

24

4) Men need to develop better fathering skills in order to offer their children a different picture of manhood and an opportunity to avoid repeating their own fathers' violence.

Summary

The effort to explain why some men are particularly violent against women has lead to many theories. These tend to fall into three major categories suggesting that violence is primarily an outgrowth of:

1) individual psychological factors;

2) family problems; or,

3) a combination of psychological and social problems.

While all these are helpful to some degree, the theories taken alone have many contradictions. The family theories imply that the woman provokes the violence, and the combination theories imply that an overwhelming variety of causes are involved.

The *failed macho complex* shows how the batterer's psychological deficiencies are a reaction to the social pressures of the male sex role. It suggests that men are violent in response to their perceived inadequacies as men, and the efforts to be the men they think they should be. In other words, certain men are more violent if they see themselves as not living up to the male sex role. In short, the beliefs men have about how men and women should feel, think and behave need to be changed in order to stop the violence – and keep it stopped.

Chapter 3

What Sets Him Off?

Violent men are not always violent. This makes it particularly difficult to live with them. A woman can end up in terror, not knowing from one minute to the next when her husband or lover will turn violent. This uncertainty can be as tormenting as the violence itself. So, many abused women look for a pattern to the violence in order to anticipate and avoid it. But too often there is no pattern. Women are left wondering what sets them off? Is there anything in particular that triggers the violence?

Yes, there are usually identifiable things that set a man off, but they are usually in the man's perception of things and not in the things themselves. This leaves a woman with little prospect of trying to effectively manage or contain the violence on her own.

THE TRIGGER

According to some psychologists, violence is triggered by a combination of what our environment presents and our reactions. This is not a direct cause and effect relationship. In other words, saying something against your husband or lover doesn't alone cause him to be violent. In fact, there is much truth to the adage: "No one can make another person do anything." The process is one where a man has choices each step of the way. Many men have been taught, however, to limit these choices to those provided in the male sex role. This is suggested in these comments:

"I always hated myself for being abusive and swore I would never be that way. I always made the excuse that she made me do it. I did know deep down inside that I was wrong, but I gave myself permission to do it anyway."

The steps to a violent incident might be outlined as follows:

1. Something occurs that may or may not be meant as a conflict.

2. The batterer perceives the event as threatening.

3. The batterer experiences some physical arousal in the form of tension or agitation.

4. The batterer then labels the arousal as anger or anxiety.

5. The batterer finally chooses to act on that anger violently.

At steps two, four and five the batterer chooses how he will respond. The violence, in this light, is not automatic.

EXPECTATIONS AND CHOICES

At step number two the batterer could decide that the event is not threatening. Violence would be avoided. Unfortunately, given the high expectations of the male sex role, simple events are readily interpreted as a threat to manhood. Simply serving dinner late can be perceived as an affront to a man's sense of privilege and power. Of course, many things well beyond the influence of the woman can inflate or deflate his expectations and become threatening in step number two. A bad day at work, for instance, can distort his perceptions further while the stress heightens his tension and agitation. "I come home from work so 'wired' some days that a whisper could set me off," explains one batterer.

At step number four, the batterer could label his arousal as a feeling other than anger or anxiety. He could see himself as feeling hurt, sad, confused, or frustrated. But conforming to the male sex role, he is more likely to label it anger. This is in fact more often the only emotion men will allow themselves to have. They tend to consider other emotions as feminine, and therefore a sign of weakness. Allowing other feelings to be explored or expressed at this point would also deflect the violence. A batterer in a counseling program explains it this way:

29

"Being angry was the easy way out. When you get angry you don't have to deal with your other feelings, especially the ones of hurt or frustration. You just let it rip, plow through, and get your way with anger. You learn from a long history that it usually works for you until you finally mess things up so bad that you've got to change. You have to start to deal with a lot of feelings if you are ever going to save your family and yourself."

Last, men choose to act on their anger with aggression and violence. Men are inclined to use aggression and violence as an expedient response to feelings. We learn that it gets us what we want with a minimum amount of feeling. And it helps us maintain our privilege and power while reducing future threats.

Of course, there are many nonviolent ways to respond to anger if it does arise. But often we have to be made to see that these nonviolent alternatives can be productive, even though they take a little more effort. Simply walking away from an angry moment, as is often done in *Time Outs*, is such an alternative. (*Time Outs*, which are commonly taught to batterers as a violence avoidance technique, are discussed in Part Two.)

A HABIT OF VIOLENCE

Violence erupts so fast that it is hard to imagine that a process of choice is behind it. A common plea is:

"It was like automatic! Before I knew what happened we'd be into it. The violence just seemed to happen all by itself. It sort of took me over."

The fact is that in many cases the choices were made a long time ago. And the action of the moment is like a *habit*. According to some psychologists, repeated violence reinforces the tendency to be violent. Over time, it becomes easier and easier to be violent. Each repeated event may teach us that violence "works" in accomplishing what we intended. It stopped the perceived threat and relieved arousal.

For some men violence becomes an *addiction*. It gives them a "rush," and a feeling of power. The thrill of violence is so strong that they crave it. Then they provoke it or go looking for it. This is the case especially with the men we term "the ugly guys." As one chronic batterer stated:

"For me the pull toward violence is still there. It doesn't all of a sudden stop and it's all over. After all these years, it becomes a part of you. You can actually feel it in your body — the adrenalin, the tingle, the release, whatever. The violence becomes kind of a fix...and that's hard to let go..."

Besides becoming a fixed habit in some men, violence can also become a *playful tool*. That is, when we realize how effective violence is in asserting the privilege and power so many of us men desire, we act violent without the process of arousal and anger. We act violently as a part of our

31

role. It becomes part of us, a way of life. It is a convenient way to avoid ever having events that might dare to threaten us. It becomes the ultimate tool for control. As one man explains:

"I knew I could control every move she made. I always had to know exactly when she was coming home, if she went somewhere by herself. There were lists of things she had to do. If she didn't do them she knew that she might get it. That's how things worked."

ALCOHOL'S ROLE

Most batterers also abuse alcohol and so alcohol is often considered to be a violence trigger. The relationship of alcohol to violence is more complicated than that, however. It is best considered a reinforcer of the trigger. Alcohol acts as a reinforcer in these ways:

1) Alcohol distorts perceptions and makes it easier for a man to see events as threatening.

2) Alcohol increases arousal and makes it easier to feel angry.

3) Alcohol suppresses reasoning and thus makes violent behavior an easier choice.

In short, alcohol provides a convenient excuse to be violent. It helps men surrender responsibility for their behavior. They can always say "the alcohol made me do it." The point here is that alcohol does not make a man violent. It only allows him to think he is excused. So if a man has any doubts about his violence, taking a drink will help him get beyond those doubts and also silence them after a violent incident. According to one man, drinking even helped erase the violence from his mind:

"I have always been into a lot of drinking and drugging to solve my problems. I mean it just helps me deal with all of the hassles and pressures. But in the process, I realize now, it also put me out of touch sometimes with what was going on. I would really lose it all. In fact, I don't even remember most of the times I was supposedly violent. My mind was just a blank."

The reality is that violent men are more likely to abuse drugs and alcohol than non-batterers. But the percentage of men who abuse alcohol and are not physically violent toward women is still very high. Also, studies have shown that the drinking batterers are sober during 40 percent of the battering incidents. Furthermore, counselors report that men who stop their drinking seldom stop their violence.

One batterer remained violent during his five years in Alcoholics Anonymous, despite his efforts to stop both his drinking and his violence. It wasn't until he joined a program especially designed for women batterers that he finally ceased his violence. This may be because woman abuse is much less detrimental to self than alcohol abuse. There is often more motivation to stop the alcohol abuse because of the damage to personal health from the addiction. Woman abuse harms the woman but often gets the batterer what he wants.

TAKING RESPONSIBILITY

The answer to "What sets him off?" is "Himself." However, seldom will a man see or admit this. To do so would be to admit a weakness, to feel threatened. Part of his defense is to minimize the violence, to say "it never happened," or "it was no big deal." Another defense is to say that someone had it coming. The most frequent excuse comes in this form:

"When my wife starts bitching it just doesn't stop. She bitches about the kids, bitches about not being with the kids, bitches about too much work, bitches about me not helping enough in the basement. She bitches about bitches. There's no way to stop it. You know that can really get to you."

As mentioned earlier, there is also the defense of alcohol or anger. We blame the anger on them rather than ourselves or the victim. Probably the most baffling defense a woman is likely to hear is that men are victims too. The most common complaint counselors hear from batterers is that they have been some how "hurt" or put upon by their victims. They genuinely feel like their feelings have been hurt in a way that justifies retaliation. As one man recollects:

34

"My wife has a way with words you know. She knows how to stick the knife in there and really turn it. I just really feel backed into a corner sometimes. The only way out is to come out swinging."

This feeling of hurt is possible for two reasons. One is that the emotional state of so many men is so fragile that it does not take much to challenge them. They simply do not deal well with feelings and, in fact, avoid dealing with those feelings by acting violently. Two, the men are so oblivious to how their victim feels and the pain they cause her, that they easily inflate their own discomfort over hers.

When batterers are confronted about their "hurt," it usually turns out to be rather insignificant. An expectation was violated rather than a big emotional happening. This is a far cry, as well, from the physical harm and psychological turmoil batterers inflict on women. Part of the challenge is to get them to understand the consequences of their behavior. As one man in a counseling program said:

"I made her feel like shit. That hurt her more than punching her in the nose. All those years, I thought I was the one being abused. I thought I was right. I didn't have what I wanted, like sexual things, the relationship with a woman that I wanted to have. I never realized that I was the one creating the problems."

35

This realization begins to take shape only when a man is prompted to take responsibility for his behavior. Only when he accepts the responsibility for initiating and directing his behavior, does he regain the capacity to change it.

Summary

Men choose violence. The male sex role influences these choices, however. Men trying to live up to the male sex role are more likely to perceive even neutral events as a threat to their manhood. They are also more likely to identify their emotional arousal as anger and to act on that anger violently. While this is largely a conscious process, repeated acts of violence may turn violence into a habit or unfeeling tool of control. Alcohol, too, may intensify the violence and make it easier to occur. But alcohol is not the cause of violence, any more than anger or the victim. Men will supply many excuses to defend their violence, and the power that they get from it; but they ultimately must accept responsibility. Only in this way can they begin to choose alternatives, and thus begin to change their behavior.

Chapter 4

Will He Try To Kill Me?

Certainly one of the most urgent questions in a woman's mind is, "How dangerous is a batterer?" Chapter Three addressed the question of "when" violence is likely to occur in a relationship. This chapter addresses the concern about how serious that violence is likely to be, its *dangerousness*. The most difficult part of this concern is prediction. How does a woman know if a man is going to act on the threats he makes? How does she know whether his past abuse will escalate into life-threatening violence?

Battered women often face death threats from their batterers. On one hand, the threats appear to be part of the verbal and psychological abuse common to violent men. Therefore, they are sometimes dismissed as "hot air." On the other hand, the threats cannot be separated from the physical battering that may have occurred. They may signal the escalation of violence that is typical of many abusive relationships.

If a man batters a woman and threatens to kill her next time, it is logical to think that he will escalate the violence and do as he says. This fear has been understandably heightened by the media accounts of men who appear to have "snapped" and killed their families. The point is that it is perfectly rational to take death threats seriously, and act to assure one's safety. There are, nonetheless, other things to weigh in the process.

PREDICTING DANGER

Most professionals insist that it is next to impossible to predict dangerousness. There are too many things to consider. If this is the case, women can hardly be expected to predict the dangerousness of their batterers. So it is best to always err on the safe side. Any threats of killing, or threats of any kind of violence, should, therefore, be given the same attention as the actual violence.

Most experts believe that if there is any indication of future dangerousness, it lies in the past. The more life threatening a man's behavior has been, the more deadly he is likely to be in the future. Men who have used weapons, caused serious physical injury, committed harsh sexual assaults, and been involved with criminal activity are the most likely to escalate their violence. In other words, those batterers we labeled the "ugly guys" are the most dangerous.

While this seems logical, it is not always clear to someone living with a violent man. For one, it is difficult to challenge or leave a generally violent person. Leaving would seem to provoke further violence. Two, these men are no less involved in police arrest, counseling, or treatment than other types of batterers. Therefore, there is often the illusion that they are likely to change or curb their life-treatening behavior.

DANGER NOW

Psychologists, nevertheless, argue that we can "predict" short-term or immediate danger. Much of this is common sense rather than some power of forecasting. If a man is extremely hostile and making threats, it is highly probable that an incident will become more and more violent unless interrupted. This interruption can be brought about by the man or the woman. Predicting the most effective means of interruption becomes the hard part. Calling the police, leaving the house, getting the attention of a neighbor, or threatening divorce may alone or together interrupt the violence and head off danger. Retaliating with violence, however, tends to cause an escalation. As one batterer recalls his dangerousness:

"I was really out of control. There is no doubt about it. There were times that I really didn't know what I was doing. I would cut loose and not stop until I was exhausted. I know I hurt her real bad more than a few times — and I probably came close to killing her. I was getting worse, even though I was trying to stop the abuse. Who knows what might have happened if I had kept doing it. In my

39

case the police coming and my wife's leaving made me stop and look at what was happening. I don't know what would have happened if I had kept at it like I was...."

The point is that aggression tends to escalate into violence, and violence into deadly violence. When violence emerges, with hostility, aggressiveness, and threats, it is likely to turn into something ugly, *fast*. Violence is like a house fire. A small flame can suddenly burst into a devouring blaze. The best thing is to put out the flame while it is just flickering. Otherwise, run for cover. It is next to impossible to predict when a flame will appear. The only thing we can do is attempt to prevent fire by making sure that inflammable materials aren't near something hot. For violence, this means being alert to danger signals.

SIGNALS

There are two types of danger signals: *intention* and *opportunity*. The batterer usually expresses his intention through threats. As said before, he may also reveal his intentions through his past actions, such as trying to choke and seriously harm his wife, lover, or other people. Other strange behavior may also signal his intent. The batterer may talk of hearing voices, describe scenes of grizzly violence, or show intense depression.

Opportunity usually involves people, places, and things. The most obvious perhaps is the availability of weapons. Heavy use of drugs or alcohol is another thing that may turn a threat into an act. Probably the most important factor, and the one that women have some control over, is the accessibility to a victim. If a woman is separated from the batterer or in a shelter, the chances of the batterer acting on his threat are lessened. There are still no assurances, however. In fact, the fear of desertion may intensify a batterer's threats and desire for revenge.

FEAR OF DESERTION

Some psychiatrists and family counselors say that women incite violence and even put themselves into dangerous situations. With the large number of violent men and the general degradation of women, it is hard to accept the popular notion that "women ask for it." It is like looking for what a prisoner in a concentration camp did to deserve being there. The issue really should be, "What do the guards do to people who try to escape and regain their freedom?" The guards may even be somewhat benevolent as long as a prisoner remains passive. Trying to escape brings on a deadly reaction, though.

So it is with many violent men. Their greatest fear is that the woman in their lives will try to desert them. To men with a sense of male power and privilege, this can be the final insult. Without someone to rule or control, they have no power. And many men in programs report they need someone to take care of them. They count on their wives or lovers for food, washing clothes, taking care of the kids, and cleaning the house. They also depend on their

41

wives or lovers for emotional support. Wives or lovers have often done much of their feeling for them. Without the women in their lives, they are at a loss. Many violent men, therefore, feel suddenly isolated if their wives or lovers leave for shelter or separation. Being alone can be frightening for some of these men. It means having to look hard at one's self. What they see they don't like.

According to another man's hindsight:

"It was pretty scary for me when my wife and kids left. I was really alone for the first time in my life. I did feel lonely a lot of the time. And I wasn't really taking good care of myself. I probably really don't know how. I was really angry about it at first. I was 'raring' to go get her and bring her back. 'How dare she leave me!' I thought. If I could have got my hands on her I would have made her pay. But I'm starting to see things differently now. It took some time alone and a lot of work though."

Summary

Women want to know the answer to "How dangerous is he?" However, most experts agree that it is next to impossible to tell for sure. It is safest to assume the worst, even though women in abusive relationships often want to assume the best. The strongest danger signal may be past violence. "Generally violent men" are the most likely to be deadly, and it is therefore especially important to separate from them. Also, serious violence is more likely to result from an escalation of a hostile or violent incident.

This is especially true if weapons and alcohol are present. It seems that leaving the violent situation may sometimes incite further violence. Violent men tend to fear desertion. But the victim has no control over her partner's fear. Her leaving confronts the man with the need to change.

Chapter 5

A Woman's Story

No two battered women have the same story. Each experiences a unique combination of abuse, fear, and uncertainty. Nevertheless, there are shared experiences. Nearly all battered women face confusion and self-doubt, yet feel cautious hope. While the following story may not be your own, it illustrates these common reactions to violent men. It reminds us of the barriers to ending the violence, and also of the courage of so many to work at it.

"I don't know when or how it all started. There had been flare-ups now and then. My husband and I would argue over the baby or not having sex, but usually I'd just give in and things would blow over. All couples have fights like this, or so I thought. The disagreements seemed part my fault anyhow. But it's true we didn't talk seriously much beyond that.

Then, one day early-on in our marriage, my husband hauled off and hit me over nothing. It was just after dinner and he started making something of my not cleaning up the house. I don't even remember saying anything back to him. I might have started to ask a question.

He slapped me backhanded across the face and then shoved me up against the wall. That's what really hurt. And those eyes! He looked like he could have killed me if I moved an inch the wrong way. I didn't dare say anything more about it. I just let the whole matter lie, hoping it would pass.

Later that night, my husband acted like it never happened and was all sweet and nice. It wasn't long, though, and he was putting me down for little things. I would occasionally talk back. That's what a person is supposed to do to a lie. But it wasn't worth it. My husband would get that look and I was frightened that he'd start hitting me again. Then he did. I think it was next after an argument over the baby. And then he hit me again...and again.

It got to the point that I didn't know what to expect. Sometimes he would be real apologetic and make up to me, and then we'd have a few good and tender moments. Then other times he would blame it all on me and threaten to hit me again if I acted up. I felt like I was in a cage or something. One false move and I'd get punished.

Now I know that my husband had some bad experiences growing up and sometimes has tough days at work. At first, I thought that I must have been adding to his problems. I thought some of the abuse might be my fault for not being a better or more supportive wife. But when I heard about

46

other abused women, I began to think maybe it was not just me. After all, my husband would go off sometimes for no reason, no matter what I did or did not do.

The abuse seemed to get worse instead of better, like I had hoped. My husband kicked me one time, in the back, and I could hardly walk for a week. I shoved him back in desperation, and he went crazy screaming and punching and throwing things until I ran out of the house. I stayed overnight that time with a relative but came back because I was worried about the kids. He was getting on them more and more and hit one with a baseball bat one day.

Why didn't I leave for good? I always thought my husband would change. I thought too that we were married, and I'd be the failure if I didn't make a good home. As it turns out he was impossible to please.

The funny thing is that my husband thinks *I* abused *him*. As I said, I occasionally asked him questions or tried to challenge his put downs, and he'd turn it all around like I was attacking him. And sure there were times I would scream or yell at him...I mean, I was scared for my life, or simply tired of being run into the ground. It got to me. I was feeling constant tension and depression, and I would snap sometimes.

Also, I admit there were moments when I knew I was going to get hit. I could see him in that rigid mood. It would fill the whole house. So I would press at him a little to get it over with. Words were the only defense I had...he's so much bigger and stronger than I am. You have to do some things just to survive or help the kids survive. I don't mean that I'd think all this out; that's just the way it happened on occasion.

I didn't know what to do for the longest time. I couldn't talk to my husband about the abuse or he'd threaten me or get angry. I had lost so much self-esteem anyway that I didn't care some of the time. Then, finally, one day I saw the terror in the kids' faces during a blow-up and knew I had to do something for them, if not me.

A friend of mine told me about a marriage counselor. I set up a counseling session to help me, and with the counselor's insistence brought my husband. He went once and then canceled the other appointments. I almost called the police a couple of times, and even threatened to do so once, but felt that would just cause more problems.

Finally, I went to a women's shelter with the kids after one particularly bad incident. My husband called the shelter saying it wouldn't happen again. The kids wanted to go home after a day or so, too. I returned, but it was a mistake.

When I finally talked about divorce, and called a lawyer for advice, my husband agreed to get some help. He went to a special men's program for about a month or so. Then he told me he was O.K. and stopped going. It did seem that things had settled down a bit. But then he started saying I was testing him. He claimed that I didn't love him or trust him enough. After all, he insisted, he had changed. It was all my fault now.

I have been living at a relative's for a few months, since finally leaving for real. My husband still wants me to come back, but I am just too scared and confused about it all at this point. Sure I still feel some love for him, and I want the kids to know their father. But I have some bitterness over all that has happened between us, too. And I need some time to sort that out. I need some time for my wounds to heal. Not so much wounds on the outside, but those on the inside."

Source: Gondolf & Russell, *Man to Man: A Guide For Men In Abusive Relationships,* Bradenton, FL: Human Services Institute, 1987, pp. 45-47.

Part Two

His Chances

Chapter 6

Will He Ever Change?

The question women most often ask about a violent man is, "Will he, *can* he, change?" Many battered women want to see the violence stopped and still maintain their relationship. So women's concern for change in men is particularly strong. What the change question may actually mean is, "Can I expect the violence to stop without having to end the relationship?" Ending a relationship has hardships of its own. But those hardships are not insurmountable and may be easier to deal with than the hardship and *uncertainty* of waiting for change.

THE PUZZLE OF CHANGE

Change has been a very popular subject in recent years. There are countless books, for instance, about the recovery process in alcoholic men. Most clinicians and researchers say that the change process defies common sense. That is, how and why people change often contradicts what we might expect. Here are some of the contradictions those working to change batterers see:

1) A man must be more concerned with *how he is abusive* and *why he should stop*, than *why he abuses* and *how he should stop*.

2) The most helpful thing a battered woman may do for a violent man is leave him.

3) A long-term commitment to change will shorten the time it takes to get results.

4) If a man thinks or says he is cured, he probably isn't.

5) Becoming non-violent may at first increase a man's psychological or verbal abuse.

6) There are no shortcuts to change, only shortfalls.

These rules or principles all imply that change does not happen suddenly. They suggest that change is a long-term process. In fact, change may be a life-long commitment to daily efforts. Some men, as we suggested earlier, may be "addicted" to their violence, similar to an alcoholic's addiction to drinking. Change in this case means becoming committed to a whole new set of beliefs and values, that is, a completely new lifestyle.

One man reflects on his efforts to change:

"It hasn't been easy by any means for me. It is a long hard process with some slips and falls along the way. I have to think about it every day. It's (the abuse) been such a part of your life for so long it doesn't suddenly go away. You have to think about how and what you are going to do this day to be different and stay different from the past. You have to really change the way you think and what you expect and how you treat other people. But I can at least look back now and say I've come a long way."

EVIDENCE OF CHANGE

How do you tell if a man is truly changing? There must be evidence that a man is acting differently in many parts of his life, not only in his abusiveness. Some of the important questions to ask are:

1) Is the man openly concerned about the woman's safety and the safety of the children? Does he take concrete steps to assure their safety?

2) Does he permit the woman to get help and support, to do what she finds necessary to feel safe?

3) Does he regularly attend any program for personal change, like a batterers program, counseling sessions, Alcoholics Anonymous, or church activities?

4) Is the man associating with different friends, those who clearly do not support or reinforce violence against women?

5) Is the man less rigid, critical, manipulative, and demanding?

6) Does he acknowledge the woman's feelings and rights, and admit more openly his wrongs and limitations?

In sum, change is evident not in words but in action.

THE PROCESS

Another basic misconception about change is that it happens either as steady, gradual progress or as some overnight conversion. A woman can be deeply disappointed if she expects too much, too soon. Often, men who are trying to change will claim that they are "different." It is common, in fact, to hear them insist after some short-term intervention that they are "cured." And often they are convinced that they are. Or men will argue that all their little changes add up to a new person. There may be some isolated good things that a man has done, but they hardly mean that he has quelled his violent tendencies. In either case, a man is revealing his ignorance of the difficulties in making change. As one batterer explains his quitting a batterer program:

"I got things under control now, or so I thought. I had been on my good behavior for over a month. And I was learning things about how to take 'time outs' and cool off rather than constantly fight back. But I found out the hard way I couldn't control anything. That was the problem. I just thought that I could 'will' my way through it...just sort of bite my tongue; but I found out the hard way I was wrong."

The change process is more a series of big steps, or stages. It is very easy to stop at any one step and think that it's all there is. It is also very likely that the stages of change will look rather bumpy and uncertain, and they may well be. Careful studies of people who have changed reveal many slips, stumbles, and spurts that gradually smooth out. These ups and downs make it hard to tell if a real change has taken place, or whether a man is being his old self.

STAGES

Change generally occurs through three successive stages: *realization*, *behavior change*, and *personal change*. It takes even the most receptive men nearly a year to move through the first two stages. It can take many more years to make headway in the third stage. At first, violent men tend to be caught in a state of emphatic denial. They either justify or downplay their violence against women, or both. The world centers around them. In fact, people around them tend to be viewed as objects for their pleasure. "Survival-of-the-fittest," "dog-eat-dog," or "me-against-the-world" is usually what they believe. One batterer puts it this way:

"You couldn't tell me a damn thing. I thought it (the violence) was all her fault. And what I did do was not that big a deal. That's just 'the way things are.' I mean it was just normal for men to be like that, tough and aggressive. Really, I didn't think I had much choice. The world is a pretty tough place and if you don't do it to them, they will do it to you. So if anybody tried to tell me anything different, I thought they were full of it...and told them as much."

Realization

The first stage of change is *realization*. In the realization stage, a man begins to think that he has done something wrong; not so much wrong in the moral sense but in the practical sense. He begins to realize that it is not in his best interest to be abusive or violent. This message is usually conveyed in terms of authority or restraint, in other words, something that beats him at his own game. A man in this stage is likely to be most responsive to arrest or jailing, separation or divorce. According to another batterer:

"I think I started to wake up when my wife left. I knew then that I had destroyed the relationship. I'd had an 'order of protection' filed against me and she was threatening to get a divorce. It had been coming. I knew things were pretty bad, but then it all hit me. I realized my life was really messed up

at that point. And I had to do something about it. I had to do something to take away some of the pain and frustration."

Eventually, the batterer realizes that aspects of his behavior must be changed for his own good. He stops the denial by admitting to others his responsibility for his violence and becomes willing to make some changes, even if it's just to get his wife or partner back or the police off his back. This moves him toward the second stage.

Behavior Change

In this stage, a batterer begins to manage his behavior for his own self-interest. He makes an effort to do some things differently in order to minimize his problems. At first, the resistance to a hard look at self is strong. The preoccupation is with controlling external acts. Gradually, a man discovers that there are feelings behind the behavior that have to be changed, too. As he begins to respond to his feelings and redirect them, he develops some empathy for others' feelings. The result may be that he sees the world as a collection of many people that have to be considered, not just himself. A batterer discusses his change this way:

"I like the way the men's program (a counseling program for batterers) made me become aware of my own feelings. Learning that I could cry and become a friend opened me up. I recognized the need to have love and friendship. Also, if I have stress building, I have to relieve it. It made me

59

recognize levels of tension that I never paid any attention to before...."

A group counseling or supervised self-help program is usually essential to promoting and sustaining this stage of change. Unfortunately, most programs for batterers have a high drop-out rate. It seems that the transition to this stage of change is especially tough or that enough is not done to assure a transition from the first stage. Change for many men stops at this point.

Why? It is common for a man to substantially lessen his violence after three months to six months in a counseling or batterer program. He is inclined to be satisfied with this and so he stops. In fact, the prospects of further change might appear to him downright scary or overwhelming. It may seem like putting his whole sense of manhood "up for grabs."

Personal Change

A few men press on for further change, change that truly makes a difference in their lives and the lives of others. Their feelings suggest to them that there's more to being a man than being tough, rigid, or domineering. In fact, as they let go of some control, they experience a sense of relief and find new potential. Some say this is when they start to feel better about themselves, and begin to examine themselves more closely. In the process, they begin to question old values and beliefs about men and women. And at some point they start to alter their own self-concept. One of these few men talks of his change this way:

"I did find out that I should try to make my life the way I wanted it to be, not the way anybody else wanted it to be. I should do it fair and square instead of through being demanding. I am trying to make my life as I want it to be by showing my wife that she is my equal. I haven't accomplished that yet, but I'm working on it."

Support that goes beyond an instructional-type batterer program is usually needed to prompt and sustain this level of change. Individual or family counseling, some type of support group, or a service activity may be appropriate. As a man undergoing personal change, he needs a way to confirm his new self and pay some penance for his old self. He needs a new group of friends that allow and encourage him to become someone new. This stage is one that too few reach for, and one that may seem hopelessly remote for violent men. But, there is a growing number of men who are working at "putting on the new man." As one man summarizes his course of change:

"To stand up and be responsible. That is being a man. I don't mean going out and working eight hours and bringing a paycheck home. I don't mean punching out other men and having people scared of you. I think being a man is being able to do everything in life: Being able to cook, wash, sew, be a provider, speak your peace, eliminate violence... that is what I am working on. Getting your point across

without being a bully. To me that's a man. It's not a one-sided thing. I once thought that the man ruled the house and everyone listened. That's not it. Being happy is being a man."

Summary

Whether a man is changing or will change is difficult to know for several reasons. Change often appears as a paradox in that it goes against some of our common sense notions about how change ought to occur. Some hard and fast evidence of different actions and attitudes is necessary to prove that real change is happening. Change among violent men is definitely a long-term process, not a quick conversion nor straight forward progress. In fact, it can best be characterized as a series of stages that take a man from a state of denial to a change in self-concept. Different interventions are appropriate at different times to help sustain the change. While few men as yet face up to the demands of this process, it is clearer each day that it is an ideal "whose time has come."

Chapter 7

Will It Get Worse Before It Gets Better?

Both women and men hope that wanting to change means the start of something better. It can, of course, but more than likely there is still a bumpy road ahead. Things may get worse before they get better. Even under the best circumstances change doesn't happen overnight or smoothly. It is accompanied by many adjustments, close calls, and even relapses. These are discouraging and can raise suspicions and fears. Knowing some of the difficulties of change can be helpful in sorting out whether the bad times are just more of the same abuse pattern or the remnant of a dying past.

HIGH HOPES AND FALSE PROMISES

Change is always inflated with high hopes and false promises. When a violent man finally makes an effort to change, his wife or mate often feels some relief and hope. At last he is going to do something about his violence! In fact, women in shelters are much more likely to return to a husband or lover once he joins a counseling program. This is regardless of how dangerous the man is and how independent or financially well-off she is. The man's slightest positive step is taken as a major leap.

Similarly, the man is quick to make big promises. Some men joining a program, especially those who have worked through their denial, will vow to attend every meeting and do whatever it takes to stop their violence. Their enthusiasm is very convincing and may be, for the most part, sincere. A man's violence may appear to subside, and his attitude become more positive. But he is quick to use this as leverage against the woman. "Come back to me now that I've changed!" is the plea.

If the woman returns too soon, the man often looses his incentive to change. The promises then turn out to be false. Relapses occur, or at least "close calls" in which the man approaches being violent but stops with verbal and psychological abuse. The man appears to be "willing" his way into different behavior. He may rely heavily on techniques like "time outs" or simply "gritting his teeth." Obviously, he hasn't changed much in terms of the stages discussed in the previous chapter.

A man in this situation is similar to the overweight dieter who tries to curb his eating. Before long, the dieter binges, stuffing himself all at once. If deeper personal change isn't accomplished, he is likely to start and stop diets again and again. So is a changing abuser likely to vacillate in his behavior, until he makes more substantial personal change.

In other words, what a violent man does after a relapse, not the relapse itself, may be the key evidence of his change. If a man seeks outside help, assures the woman's safety, and takes new precautions, then things may eventually get better.

NONVIOLENT TERRORISTS

One other thing that may make change seem *worse* at first is the terrorism that continues and perhaps even heightens. Some violent men stop their violence only to become "nonviolent terrorists." They try to get their way, maintain their control, and act powerful by using more threats, abusive language, and verbal manipulations.

A batterer may be on what substance abuse counselors term a "dry drunk." That is, even though a man has no alcohol, the man still acts like an alcoholic. Even when nonviolent, a batterer may act like a violent man. To compensate for the lack of violence, he may commit more psychological or verbal abuse.

Any victim of terrorism will be momentarily grateful that the violence has stopped, even while still held captive. But the captivity or the threats are still abuse and deserve to be challenged. In fact, nonviolent abuse needs to be challenged the same way as physical abuse. This is hard to do, not only because of the tendency to relax amidst the nonviolence, but also because of the self-pity and self-congratulations expressed by a man who is acting nonviolently.

SELF-PITY

Often men who claim they are trying to change fall into self-pity that makes things worse, at least for a while. They feel put upon, unappreciated, and mistrusted. Some of this may be a reflection of depression. Losing some control is discouraging. Also, facing previously repressed emotions can be disturbing. The man may experience moments of anxiety, and disillusionment. As one batterer put it:

"There were times I just wanted to drive head-on into a tree. I felt like nothing was going right for me. No matter what I did, or how hard I tried it didn't seem to make a difference. There was no way she was going to come back to me or trust me. The kids are even bad mouthing me behind my back. I hate myself for not doing something about my abuse four or five years ago, before it was too late."

It is typical to revert to a lot of blame at this point. Men who recognize their abusiveness may also become aware of the social forces contributing to it. They may start to see themselves as victims of the faults inherent in the male sex role. They may see their fathers or mothers as abusive to them as children. And women may appear to them as pointing the finger while getting all the support.

Another man notes:

"It is not all that easy being a man either, you know. Look, we have a lot of stuff heaped on us,

too. You have to be responsible, look after money, and keep the kids in line. That's not all fun and games. It's pretty hard to change all that. In fact, there are a lot of pressures that just won't change. You have to put up with them. I mean, after all, that's part of life."

All this self-pity can amount to more denial. While some of the self-pity may be understandable, it can set the stage for relapse or stalled change. The awareness it signals, however, can be positive if it is pointed toward more concern about the experience of the victim than self. Weighing one's self-pity against the harm done to others may be the start of moving on. One man suggests this sort of reevaluation:

"I know that I may feel down at times or even a little hurt, but it's nothing compared to what I've put her through. I mean I devastated her, and that's nothing that is going away over night. That's what I really feel bad about now...what I managed to do to her."

SELF-CONGRATULATIONS

Another extreme that complicates the change process is self-congratulations. If a man manages to stop his violence even for a short while, he feels he deserves credit for it. As one man says:

"I have really put myself out. I've been going to counseling and doing the things they teach us there. I have stopped short of getting violent several

67

times just in the last couple of weeks. My drinking is down too. And what do I get from her? The same thing. Nothing really can satisfy her. Here I am putting out all this effort. I think I deserve something – I mean some 'thanks' – in return."

Many men, in fact, are likely to consider themselves cured at this point. They will very openly celebrate this belief. In the man's view, he thinks he is doing something great and is very impressed with himself. He has made a great sacrifice in stopping his violence. He may talk about how he has given up his power to suppress his wife or partner. He sees himself now having to take her nagging, with his hands tied.

Battered women are, however, understandably reluctant to trust or accept the violent man at this point. Often a woman has taken tremendous risks to expose her batterer's abuse or to challenge it to the extent that he was willing to seek help. Now, he suddenly wants her approval and congratulations.

Suspicion, or at least caution, is wise, given all the shortcomings and difficulties of change. A woman may well further challenge a man for his verbal abuse or his inflated promises. In his self-congratulations, a man may consider this "testing." He is likely to complain that his wife or lover doesn't trust him and constantly tries to trip him up to see if he has really changed. That may be true, but the man has to appreciate why this is so.

ACCEPTING THE INEVITABLE

Men attempting to become nonviolent must inevitably accept two things. First, his relationship may never be what it was or what he would like it to be. Violence may have damaged it beyond repair. Testing one's mate is a necessary precaution that may never end. The only one who will congratulate a man for his progress may be himself. As one man admits:

"I first started coming to counseling to try to save my marriage. I thought I would come here a few times and they'd see what I was talking about and tell me how to fix it all up. I began to see, though, that it doesn't work that way. I had some changes I had to make in myself. That was the only way things would ever get better around me. Not when I was trying to change or fix everybody else, but when I took care of myself. I'm going to the counseling group now for myself."

A man on a subway wouldn't be inclined to thank a person who stepped on his foot for getting off it. His foot shouldn't have been stepped on in the first place. So it is with violence: a man cannot expect thanks and praise for not doing something he should never have done in the first place, especially since much of the fear and control lingers on.

A second thing a man needs to accept in order to move beyond self-congratulations is that change, as has been discussed, is a continuing process, not a

69

terminal state. He cannot rest on his small accomplishments, as tempting as that may be. Rather, he has to use them as stepping stones to more substantial change. The minute a violent man thinks he can relax, he is likely to lapse into old patterns of thought and behavior. Like a security guard, he must learn to stay alert. Self-congratulations go against that. It gets him looking too much at the moment, rather than ahead to the future.

Summary

Efforts to change may bring with them extreme uncertainty and disappointment. There are the woman's high hopes and the man's false promises. The man is likely to make commitments he is unable to keep. He doesn't realize what it takes for him to change and he wants to regain his wife's or partner's approval.

Several events may appear to make things worse. Changing men often become nonviolent terrorists. They may temporarily become more verbally abusive in compensation for restraining their physical abuse. Second, they may develop self-pity and even blame the woman in order to ease their "pain."

Third, such men will probably express self-congratulations, expecting the women to stop "testing" them and embrace them for their efforts to change. Any of these can be stumbling blocks to a genuine change. But if a man realizes that he cannot expect the relationship suddenly to be "repaired," and that he has a long way to go, things will eventually get better instead of worse.

Chapter 8

Does Counseling Work?

Violent men are now entering counseling programs more than ever before. Most major cities across the country have a long-term batterer program, and an increasing number have short-term court-mandated programs. The question most women raise about this trend toward counseling is "Does it work?" Or, should these programs be viewed as just another false promise.

Given what's been said about the change process, there is room for doubt. The outcome of counseling programs is not clear-cut. While the creation of counseling programs is an encouraging sign of a growing recognition that violent men should be stopped, they alone aren't enough. The question is, therefore: "What combination of interventions is required to produce and sustain genuine change in violent men?"

TYPES OF PROGRAMS

One reason it is hard to judge counseling programs is that there are so many different kinds. Among the over two hundred programs offering some form of counseling for batterers, no two are identical. Diverse approaches and formats exist. One broad classification of programs distinguishes between these types: skill-building programs, anger management programs, guided discussion programs, and anti-sexist programs. Combinations of these approaches within a single program also exist. Each approach has its own strengths and weaknesses.

Skill-building programs lead men through a series of class exercises that teach them new skills. The idea is to make up for the men's deficiencies in several areas. Men are taught how to communicate better, how to relax and reduce stress, how to get in touch with their emotions, and how to negotiate and settle conflict. One shortcoming of skill-building programs is that they often fall short of promoting the long-term commitment to change described in this book.

Anger management programs emphasize techniques for recognizing when one is getting angry, and how to interrupt or redirect that anger before in turns into violence. They spend much time teaching men how an abusive incident develops, and how to recognize the internal cues leading up to such incidents. Men also learn to identify the things that provoke or "set them off," and how to avoid them. A criticism of anger control programs is that they are often taken by violent men as a "quick fix" to their deep-seated problems.

Guided discussion programs are similar to self-help groups. Men may begin by discussing the events of their week and move to their attempts to avoid abuse. In these guided discussions, the men encourage and challenge one another to do better. The group leader may identify a topic, like "making excuses," and move the discussion toward that. Guided discussions, however, can easily wander into blaming that reinforces abuse.

The *anti-sexist programs* focus on assuring the woman's safety and undoing the male sex role stereotype. Much time is spent exposing all the forms of privilege and power exerted by the man, and getting him to take responsibility for his violence. Various exercises are used to challenge the men's distorted sense of manhood and reveal alternative roles. Anti-sexist programs are sometimes accused of slighting the immediate practical needs of men.

PROGRAM FORMATS

Besides these different approaches, there are also different program formats. For instance, there are individual counseling, couple counseling, group counseling, and class-like sessions. Most of the programs for batterers use a group format. This format seems to be the most effective in breaking down a man's denial and sustaining his change. Some more developed programs use a combination of formats. They may start with one or two individual counseling sessions followed by a class-like session, group counseling, and eventually some couple counseling, provided the wife or lover is willing.

A batterer program may work closely with a women's shelter, or be formally affiliated with one. It may be supported by a family service agency or community mental health agency. Violent men will often be referred to private counselors, substance abuse treatment, psychiatric care, or marriage counseling, instead of to a formal batterer program. While these forms of counseling may be better than nothing, they may be too unfamiliar with woman abuse to decisively address the violence. They may even overlook it.

Finally, different time spans exist among programs. Most court-mandated programs consist of twelve, weekly, two-hour sessions. Many experts believe, however, that twelve weeks is only enough time to interest a man in a longer commitment to a voluntary program. Most voluntary programs require a six- to eight-month commitment.

The more developed batterer programs operate in phases and expect a man to join a self-help or support group after eight months of class instruction, skill-building sessions, and guided discussions. The longer the program the greater the drop-out rate, but the more substantial the change for those remaining. Once a man finishes four sessions he is usually good for at least four months participation. But those who make it beyond that are still few in number.

SUCCESS RATES

The "success rates" of programs vary widely. Even the notion of what is meant by success can be unclear. Success, in terms of batterer programs, usually refers to a man remaining nonviolent for some period of time after the program. The problem is that few programs can keep in touch with ex-participants for a long enough time after the program ends to know what happens to them. The reports of other kinds of abuse are often unrecorded or unverified. And too often success rates are calculated without considering the number of drop-outs during and before the program.

Some of the better evaluations of programs suggest that about two-thirds of the men formally enrolling in a program finish, and about one-third of these men remain nonviolent after the program. Some of these ex-participants remain nonviolent because they are separated from their wives or lovers. Some have also maintained their contact with a program or support group. If the number of nonviolent men is weighed against all those who initially contacted the program but never joined, success rates drop to about ten percent.

The point is that success is hard to measure. Be suspicious of a program that boasts a sure success. There are few truly scientific evaluations of programs for violent men and even those few still have difficulty tracking down program completers to determine "success." Success, too, is difficult to define. As we have seen, there is more to success

75

than stopping violence in the short-term. It is hard for even the experts to chart out the change process and measure whether it is well under way.

MOTIVATION

One thing is certain: counseling programs do not change men in and of themselves. There is always that elusive element, motivation, that has a lot to do with change. Most changing men will tell you that stopping violence was something they alone had to make up their minds about. A typical remark is: "You have to make up your mind to do it yourself. Nobody else can do it for you."

This is not to minimize the role of counseling. Nevertheless, success may be determined as much by the willingness or responsiveness of a particular man as by format or approach. And this motivation is most likely to appear in what we termed the sporadic batterers, and is least likely in the generally violent batterers.

Men readily and earnestly acknowledge the positive role of counseling, but often not in the ways we'd expect. The most important thing from their perspective is the contact with other men like themselves. As one man explains:

"The program helped me to know that I am not alone. I find the men in the group to be basically decent people. And I found out that I am a good person, too! I have been able to get a lot of self-esteem out of that realization."

Another man adds:

"I was able to remember everybody's face in the group, remember why I was going there, and that's kept me going through tough times. If I couldn't handle something with my wife, I got the hell out of the room. I still practice this now and think about that group of men I was with."

For some violent men, a counseling group presents an alternative to their past violence; a group unlike buddies at bars, work and sports who encourage or excuse violence. Nevertheless, a man may occasionally get sympathy for his complaints or self-pity in a counseling group, even with a counselor present. He may also insist on trying out newfound feelings or techniques with his wife or lover. In no case, however, is the woman obligated to accept this. If she feels the least bit uneasy about the man's talk or use of the group, she should tell him and the program staff. The group itself is the place to practice the new skills and check one another.

Personal motivation and group involvement play an important role in "successful" change. Research shows, however, that it is not these alone that make a difference. A combination of interventions and sanctions (negative pressures) go into stopping violence. Perhaps the most successful combination is arrest followed by court-ordered counseling, and then voluntary group counseling. These interventions do not occur in a vacuum. The women's threats, police calls, shelter visits, separation, and court proceedings all play a part. A major study on this subject suggests that the more different kinds of sanctions from a woman and the community, the greater a man's chance of stopping the violence. There doesn't appear to be any magic formula, only the message that the woman "meant business" and was backed up by the community.

POLICE ARRESTS

Much publicity has been given to the effectiveness of arresting batterers. Arrest has been shown in one major study to deter violence to some degree. There remains, however, some question whether the arrest works best with certain kinds of men, and whether its effects last very long. Arrest followed by participation in a counseling program appears to be the most effective in stopping the violence.

While the number of arrests being made under mandatory arrest laws has increased, there is still an uneven response by police. Police tend to arrest men who are unruly or troublesome to them when they arrive at a house. The men who flee the house or are calm when the police arrive are less likely to be arrested, even though they may have been severely abusive. In other words, the generally violent men are most likely to be arrested, but they are also the least likely to be responsive to counseling or further intervention.

Police intervention, like counseling, is not an end in itself. Still, it plays an important role in confronting a man with the consequences of abuse. It can also play an important part in initiating and maintaining change. A man may in fact be in and out of programs and face many police calls and separations before any real change is evident. One batterer admits, like many others:

"I have had a lot of things happen to me. They all seem like a blur now. I've gone to couples counseling and private counseling. I've had 'orders of protection' thrown against me and been arrested. My wife and kids have left and she filed for divorce. I've been in detox, too. It has taken that and much more though to get me on the right road and keep me there."

Violence against women cannot be solved by merely a "get tough" attitude from police. It is a deep-seated social problem that requires a response from everyone affected, including the entire community.

Summary

Successful counseling programs depend on several things. First, there are many different kinds of program approaches and formats. Those most likely to sustain the changes described in this book are the anti-sexist programs using a group counseling format and working closely with shelters. Second, there are many factors to consider in measuring success. The most reliable program studies are those that keep track of men for a year or more after the program and consider the program dropout rate along with those they cannot reach after the program. Such studies are the exception, so it is necessary to be wary of most reported "success rates."

Third, the man's motivation, the type of batterer he is, and the combination of interventions he experiences are important factors in stopping violence. These are seldom acknowledged in calculating program success rates. Lastly, police arrests play a particularly influential role in stopping violence but, alone, can hardly be considered certain or sufficient. Counseling programs do work for some men, but generally only when they are accompanied by intervention and sanctions from the battered woman and the community at large. Counseling programs do not of themselves magically stop violence.

Chapter 9

What Can I Do To Help Him?

Many women, regardless of the violence, are interested in trying to help their husband or lover change. There are many theories about why this tendency persists, even in a situation that is dangerous and uncertain. Nevertheless, the question "What can I do to help him?" at least implies a desire to help make the relationship safer. By trying to help the man stop his violence, the woman is also asserting and protecting herself.

Given our understanding of violent behavior we are hard pressed, however, to come up with a simple answer of how to help a violent mate. The best help a woman can give to a violent man may be to appear not to help him at all. Men seem more likely to change when they perceive a real crisis that threatens their future, set in motion by the victim.

CHALLENGES

Although there is no neat profile of batterers to explain why men do what they do, there are some definite conclusion we can draw about the problem.

1) Violence against women is tied to a sense of male privilege and power, and fear of the feminine incorporated in the male sex role. While these tendencies are common to all men, there are different types of batterers who need different kinds of treatment or intervention.

2) The "failed macho complex" may best explain why some men get so violent and others are less violent. Men are more violent if they see themselves as not living up to the male sex role.

3) Men choose to act violently. Men will defend their violence — and the power they get from it — but they ultimately must accept responsibility for their behavior, if they are to change.

4) Dangerousness is difficult to predict, even for the experts. Severe violence is more likely to occur when dangerous factors, like threats, weapons and alcohol, are present, and when there has been a history of severe violence.

5)   Change in violent men is a long-term process that occurs in a series of stages. It involves a variety of interventions.

6)   A man's efforts to change are often confused by the woman's high hopes and the man's false promises. Disappointments are likely to arise from the man's non-violent terrorism, self-pity, and self-congratulations.

7)   Success in counseling programs is often misrepresented. A successful outcome is related to the program approach, the man's motivation, the type of batterer, and the combination of interventions he experiences.

Given these uncertainties and challenges, is there anything the woman can realistically do to help her violent husband or lover?

BEING FIRM

While it may seem natural for a woman to try to help a violent man, formerly battered women report from experience that this can be a trap. A woman often ends up thinking she can or is changing her batterer. In the meantime, she is probably not taking the steps that make a difference. At the other extreme, some women have tried to fight back. While fighting back may be a necessary self-defense or seem like justifiable retaliation, it is also unlikely to stop the violence. In fact, it is more likely to escalate and extend it.

According to the women in the Lee Bowker's book *Ending the Violence*, being firm on a consistent basis is essential. The violent man has to be convinced that the woman is serious. Her demands for an end to the violence have to be non-negotiable. The clearer she can be, that the violence is not her fault but is *his* responsibility, the better. And whatever threats she makes concerning leaving, calling the police, or pressing charges, they must be acted on. Acting in a caring way, or simply trying to stay calm, does not work.

The sooner a woman begins to take this stand the better, according to the research. Hoping that the violence will go away with time can be fatal. Early action, even though the violence doesn't yet seem that serious, prevents a pattern from developing. That pattern is one of escalating violence and a more dangerous situation. Men who become involved in a pattern of chronic abuse find it extremely difficult to change.

TELL EVERYONE

The more consequences and interventions a woman can call into play the better. They help back her up and give her a little more power in the relationship. This power-balancing, according to the research, tends to lessen the violence. This is understandable given how much of the violence toward women is linked to a man's "power trip."

One of the outstanding things about domestic violence is that it usually happens in isolation. Few other people, if any, find out about it. Therefore, the violent man gets away with the violence and has no reason not to repeat it. If other people or agencies are aware of the violence, they are more likely to invoke some consequences that restrain the violence and motivate the man to change.

Formerly battered women have suggested doing these things:

1) Tell family members, neighbors, friends, and clergy of any violence or threats. Encourage them to call the police if they suspect any violent incidents or threats of violence.

2) Call the police whenever violence occurs or is threatened, even if arrest is unlikely.

3) Call a shelter or women's center for advice and support, even if you do not think you are ready to leave the man, even temporarily.

4) Alert other social service agencies in your area to the violence, particularly those offering counseling, substance abuse treatment, family programs or mental health service.

85

5) Consult a lawyer about your rights pertaining to assault charges, child custody, and divorce.

Even if a woman receives no practical advice or chooses to delay acting on the advice that is given, the communication with these sources of help is important. She has put the facts on record. When she does choose to take action, it will be easier because it will not simply be the batterer's word against hers. It will be his word against hers, plus the confirmation of several other sources that know the case history. Carefully kept records, combined with police intervention, shelter stays and, if necessary, divorce, are the surest way to end the violence.

SEPARATION AND SHELTER

Often the best way for a woman to help herself and a violent man is to leave him. This was the main reason women's shelters were established. Leaving a violent man provides some immediate safety. It also gives the woman leverage if she does return to the batterer. The man's power, control and threat of violence are lessened by entering a shelter. The man learns from her shelter stay that he cannot control the woman entirely. She can leave again if endangered. It also proves the woman's assertiveness and resistance to the violence. One man's comments on the impact of shelter, echo others:

"There is no doubt in my mind that for me the change process began when my wife left. I came

86

home one night and found her gone, with a note there. She took the kids with her. I was furious, and even desperate to get her back. But it started me looking for help and realizing I wasn't going to get my way any more."

Several studies show that the leaving process is not a clear-cut end to a relationship. For many economic and emotional reasons, women tend to return to the batterer several times before a relationship is decisively ended. Even during the separations, a man finds ways to visit the woman; sometimes through promises, sometimes through fear tactics or threats, sometimes through appearances of change, sometimes through visitation rights to the children.

Leaving the violence is a difficult decision, but based on our knowledge of violence, it may be the safest recourse for a woman and the most effective means of helping a man. Violent men, as should be apparent by now, are unlikely to stop as a result of a woman's threats or because of couples counseling alone. The need to face stiff consequences and decisive interventions persist over a long period of time. Shelter stay (or other means of separation) is one such consequence and intervention.

Summary

The best way to help a violent man is to convince him that violence won't be tolerated. Although this does not insure that it will produce permanent change, it does provide for a woman's safety. A combination of consequences and interventions is required.

One step is being firm about one's opposition to the violence by following through on threats to leave and by refusing to accept the blame. A second step is to contact and inform as many family, friends, and social services agencies about any violence or threat of violence. Keep no secrets and encourage others to find out more by keeping an eye on the violent man. A third and more decisive step is to go to a shelter or separate from the batterer. Even a separation can be helpful in convincing the batterer that a woman means business and that his power and control are shrinking.

A woman facing violence needs as much reinforcement as she can muster. She should feel that she has a right to support and intervention. And hopefully her community is ready and willing to offer them to her. Stopping violent men is something we all have to do.

Chapter 10

A Man's Story

The following story portrays one man's journey from violence to nonviolence. It is certainly not the only path of change, nor necessarily the most typical. It is an exceptional story in that it comes from a man who has changed substantially, who has been transformed. Because of this man's efforts to change he is, like many of the other men cited in this book, in a position to offer some insights on what it takes to stop the violence.

"I've done just about every thing possible to my wife at sometime. We got into it almost from the day we were married. I have hit her, shoved her, forced myself on her sexually. She has gone to the emergency room because of my violence at least twice. But more than that, I've been mentally abusive pretty consistently, too.

I have controlled my wife most of the time without even knowing it or thinking about it. I just acted real rigid at times or just disregarded what she said or thought. Then there were times that I verbally put her down, or discredited what she said. Just ignoring her, you know, the silent treatment, is probably what I'm best at.

At the time, in fact for a long time, I just assumed she had it coming, or I was completely unaware that I was really being abusive. I didn't even apologize most of the time. I just acted like nothing really happened and everything would blow over. All I was concerned about was me. I wanted what I wanted, and I thought I was always right.

When I felt crossed...and with my expectations, that was easy to do...I would attack. And it wasn't just my wife or the kids. I have had my share of fights with other guys, as well. I don't really drink that much, never have. But if I was in a bar or at a party, and someone crossed me, I would go after them. Didn't matter how big they were. It was almost like instinct. I really didn't think about it that much. I just did it. Acted violent, that is.

I suppose people just thought I had a quick temper. I got angry at times, for sure. But that was just part of the whole trip of getting my way and being in control. It was all part of being stuck on myself and not really making contact with other people. The lashing out was I guess some kind of contact... the wrong kind. But it also helped me avoid my really having to open up to others, and be vulnerable, or getting hurt emotionally.

In a way, I guess I've always been afraid of opening up. I never really dealt with my feelings, until recently. I just avoided having to feel much by being violent. I just avoided getting hurt by trying to control others and keep them from doing things that might hurt me. Some of this probably started when I was young. My parents were pretty violent at times, my father especially toward my mother. And afterward he would blame it on me or on my mother. I can remember hiding under the bed as a kid when they were going at it. I know I felt hurt then, and really helpless. I wasn't going to be helpless again.

Getting beyond this came the hard way for me. My wife threatened to get a divorce after several years of abuse. She'd just had it. Also, I had some real bouts and our youngest daughter was really scarred by them. My daughter went into these tantrums that I think were the last straw for my wife. So my wife went to a shelter with the kids for awhile. And I eventually went back to live at my mother's house.

This is not the case for all other men, but for me it made a difference in my life, a difference I had to think about. Whatever I was doing obviously wasn't working. I had lost everything I had. So I had to do something different.

My wife and I had gone to a couples counselor off and on. But still I thought all the problems were her fault. Through the shelter I found out about a men's program (for batterers) and tried that. I knew at that point that I had to do something different even though I didn't know what. I thought the program could show me what I needed to do.

91

Going to the program was one of the toughest things I ever did. I put it off and put it off. In fact I think I missed my first appointment to attend. But once I got there with the other men in the group I felt OK. I began to see from them that I had a problem that in a way belonged to a lot of us. I had to accept responsibility for my behavior and for who I was. Just blaming other people and living so self-centered was destructive not only to others but also to me.

Just talking about it to others and also learning some practical things about how to deal with my attitudes and feelings, opened me up some. I began to express myself better, or in ways other than violence. That felt good for me. I realized in the process what I really thought, rather than what I thought I should think as a man.

Being different though was tough. It's still tough for me. I mean there are not many men at my work that I can talk to like I talk at the group. In fact, most of them would laugh at me, if I told them what was going on with me. I am telling more and more of them about my involvement in the program though. And they get the message that I am intent on being different.

My contact with the program has been my lifeline; the friends I met there, just having someone to really talk to. Doing something now for other men, who are where I was when I started out, is also great. It makes me feel good that I can try to help others. I need that to keep changing. And helping other guys is a way of reminding me who I really have become, or am trying to become. I think it is doing just that.

After about two years of separation my wife and I are living together again. I visited her and the kids pretty regularly over the separation. And whenever I would get uptight or ready for a fight, I would tell her and leave. I'd call her up later and, if she wanted, we'd talk about it more over the phone. It was safer for both of us that way.

But now, back in the house is a real test. I really have to watch what I'm thinking, my patterns of thought. There is so much that you just expect. A man expects certain things from a woman and vice versa. You have to constantly be putting those aside so you can really deal with each other as people.

I know that my wife still doesn't trust me fully. Or maybe it's that she is not able to forget all that happened in the past. I know it's behind me now and I am going to keep it there. I have new friends and a church group that remind me of that. I also know that I can't make my wife love me or accept me. That's not the point anymore. The point is to be a different kind of man, one who is considerate of others and who let's them be who they are. Then everything else will fall in place."

Afterword

Violence has become a daily occurrence. We seem to have a steady diet of it in TV programs, on the news, in our politics, at our schools, and in our homes. Violence, while not new to our society, has become an epidemic according to experts. The level of violence in today's world represents a general disregard for the well-being of others and oneself. It may also represent a basic disregard for life itself. Our lives may have, as some thinkers suggest, lost purpose amidst all the pulls and pushers of the modern world.

The violence of men against women, however, represents more than just a loss of purpose. It is more than a spill-over from the violent world outside the home, although that surely reinforces it. Behind much battering of women is a power struggle of a different sort: a battle of the sexes. Violence against women is part of the fear and contempt many men have for the feminine. It is a rejection of nurturing, cooperation, intimacy, tenderness, and wholeness.

Rather than let the masculine and feminine join in some complementary way that betters both sexes, many men are driven toward control, power and privilege. They expect certain things as men, and take them with force or aggression. Men have certainly become defensive about the "men bashing" of the women's movement. Some insist that the violence is not their fault and that men have to reassert some of the rights they think they are losing to women.

TOWARDS A BALANCE OF POWER

If men don't take responsibility for stopping the violence, it will continue to grow. Not only will women become even more distrustful of men, but our children will also distance themselves from us and risk abuse in their own adult lives. It is going to take "guts" for us to accept gentleness as strength amidst such a violent world.

Women, on the other hand, have been asserting greater independence. This of course represents some protection in itself. In this way, a women can more easily leave a relationship that becomes violent. She can also move into positions that challenge the privileges of men.

Diplomats argue that violence on the international scene can be stopped only through a balance of power. Only at this point are two opposing countries willing to disarm and talk with each other. A balance of power also works in the relationship between individuals. There needs to be equality and mutual respect before peace can be built. A battered woman's calling on the aid of friends, police, and social services can be a way to achieve a balance of power or at least get the attention of the batterer.

A LEAP OF FAITH

Stopping violence is more than a momentary laying down of arms. It requires a leap of faith, a conviction that violence is intolerable, unwarranted, and unjust. It has no right or excuse in the home. The faith upon which nonviolence is built also includes a belief in a power beyond ourselves. The ugly head of violence is horrifying and overwhelming for most of us. There seems little we can do about it or against it. Yet many have found the strength to not only endure violence, but to rise up against it. Battered women themselves represent survivors who have persisted and endured.

There is a courage, clarity, and power that wells up in us amidst adversity. There is a wisdom that speaks to us in quiet moments with a message of hope and direction. This strength and intelligence is there when we least expect it. It says, "Press on. Violence should not be." There is not a clear formula for how the violence will be stopped. But a way can and will be found if we commit ourselves to finding it.

Appendices

What Statistics and Shelters Say About Battered Women

by Ellen Steese

Advocates commonly quote a Bureau of Justice Statistics figure that a woman is beaten in the United States every 15 seconds. That is based on figures for the number of reported beatings that took place between 1978 and 1982.

The National Coalition Against Domestic Violence (NCADV) estimates that somewhere between 2 and 6 million women are battered each year.

(To put this in perspective, according to the Bureau of the Census in Washington, there are 97.3 million women 15 and older in the US, of which 58 million are married and living with spouse, married but spouse absent, or a partner in an unmarried couple with no other adult in the household.)

Getting out of the marriage or relationship does not guarantee protection. According to Bureau of Justice Statistics figures, in three-fourths of spouse-on-spouse assaults, the victim was divorced or separated at the time of the incident.

Battering tends to escalate over time, and homicide is sometimes the culmination. In 1986, 40 percent of all female homicide victims were killed by relatives or boy-friends.

Many statistics are based on a fairly small sample, but these still provide some interesting clues to the whole picture of domestic violence.

Women who murdered their husbands were often battered women. According to a study in Cook County (Chicago), Illinois, 40 percent of the women who committed homicides were battered women who killed their batterer.

A five-year study at Yale-New Haven Hospital concluded that 40 percent of all injury-related visits to the hospital by women were the result of battering. The study also disclosed that battering was a major precipitating factor in cases of female alcoholism and drug abuse, child abuse, attempted suicide, and situational disorders.

The children are victims, too. Not only is child abuse more likely in homes where the wife is battered, but also, children are very often witnesses to the battering. The NCADV estimates that, of these children, 60 percent of the boys will grow up to be batterers, and 50 percent of the girls will grow up to be battered women. The NCADV also estimates that in one-quarter of violent families, the wife is attacked while pregnant.

One study showed that three-fourths of all battered women reported that their abuser was not violent in public, and that they were not believed when they reported instances of brutality.

Advocates insist that emotional abuse is as devastating as physical abuse. Among the behaviors considered abusive are ridiculing a woman's beliefs or women as a group, criticizing and shouting, attempting to control, and refusal to work or to share money.

Other characteristics of a batterer include extreme suspiciousness and possessiveness, poor self-image, strongly traditional ideas about men's and women's roles, and a tendency to isolate a woman from her family or friends.

It is commonly thought that battering is largely a problem in poorer neighborhoods, but advocates insist that the problem extends across the social spectrum.

"Any woman, rich or poor, black, white, or Latina [or otherwise], could be a battered woman," says Alba Baerga, who is on the staff of Casa Myrna Vazquez shelter in Boston. Upper-class or upper-middle-class women are less likely to *report* abuse, however.

All over the US, there are shelters offering help to women who are battered. The National Coalition Against Domestic Violence, in Washington, D.C., has a toll-free hotline, 800-333-SAFE. Women who call there can get information on shelters and programs near them.

Shelters also share information. A shelter in one state, for instance, will refer a woman fleeing for her life to a shelter in another state. Some shelters in Boston offer transitional housing. And there is a long-established network in Massachusetts of "safe homes"---homes in the community that take in battered women. This is not common in most parts of the country, according to the NCADV.

Not all women who come to a shelter leave the batterer. "Some have been in shelters before," Ms. Baerga says.

103

"Some come for half an hour and decide to give another chance to the relationship. Some come determined to be independent, to find an apartment. Our main goal is to provide a safe place where they can make their own decision."

Katrina Pope, on the staff of Elizabeth Stone House, concurs. "We aren't here to say you can't go back. We're here to provide as many resources as possible, and to say there are possibilities in your life, there are options. No one deserves to be beaten."

One of the main obstacles to putting a stop to battering is that women want to deny that there is a problem.

"Some of them are strong enough to say, 'Yes, I am a battered women.' Some of them are very open about it," says Baerga. "Others are here for two months---and don't even remember they were in the shelter. It can take your whole life and you still never admit you were [battered].

"The way we measure success here: Only one phone call might be a success. It might take the woman her whole life to make that phone call."

Helping Organizations

INTRODUCTION

There are numerous organizations, both local and national, dedicated to dealing with domestic violence. Most of the national organizations provide assistance to local programs and information to persons involved in domestic violence. Most have a referral service that will direct you to the most appropriate and nearest program for help. Several toll-free hotlines are also available for crisis counseling and referral to local services (see Appendix C).

Local programs can also be found through the yellow pages of your local phone book or through directory assistance for your telephone area code. Some categories to use when looking for listings are:

> women's services,
> family services,
> social services,
> victim assistance,
> legal aid,
> alcohol and drug programs,
> rape crisis, and
> child abuse services.

Most any local social service will offer referral to the most appropriate treatment programs, as well. Don't forget that calling your local police in a crisis may be a good place to start. They should be able to refer you to appropriate shelter or counseling services, as well as intervene in a violent incident.

The main point is that *you are not alone.* There are many trained people and specialized programs available to you. Get as much help as you can from as many different organizations as you can. You not only deserve the help, but taking a variety of steps is the best way to move toward an end to the violence.

FOR WOMAN BATTERING

National Coalition Against Domestic Violence (NCADV)   202/293-8860
2401 Virginia Avenue NW, Suite 306
Washington, DC 20037

A network of women's shelter programs that provides assistance to shelters and battered women. *The Coalition* maintains a national hotline to locate the nearest shelter, and gives assistance in a crisis.

National Woman Abuse Prevention Project (NWAPP)
202/857-0216
2000 P Street NW, Suite 508, Washington, DC 20036

An information and study center with a special focus on criminal justice intervention in domestic violence cases. Publishes *Exchange*, a quarterly newsletter useful to domestic violence workers.

Ending Men's Violence Task Group   314/725-6137
c/o RAVEN, PO Box 24159, St. Louis MO 63130

A council of representatives of men's programs dealing with battering and rape, and working primarily on public awareness and social action. This group also publishes *The Ending Men's Violence National Referral Directory*. The nearest batterers program can be obtained by calling the RAVEN program at the hotline number listed in Appendix C.

Center on Women Policy Studies   202/872-1770
200 P St., NW, Suite 508, Washington DC 20036

A national clearinghouse for information, manuals, and legislation related to domestic violence. Also publishes *Response to the Victimization of Women and Children*, a quarterly journal of articles for domestic violence workers that's especially versed in the legislation of each state with regard to domestic violence.

FOR OTHER DOMESTIC VIOLENCE

National Clearinghouse on Marital and Date Rape (NCMDR) 415/548-1770
2325 Oak St., Berkeley, CA 94708

Includes access to newsletters, reports, and bibliographies on issues of marital rape. Legal consultation for marital rape cases is also available.

National Council Against Sexual Assault (NCASA)
618/398-7764
8787 State St., Suite 202, E. St. Louis, IL 62203

Offers information and advocacy for rape victims and coordination of rape crisis centers nationwide. Offers consultation and referrals to victims, as well.

National Council on Child Abuse and the Family (NCCAF) 202/429-6695
1155 Connecticut Ave NW, #400
Washington DC   20036

Provides support for local community services working against child abuse, and special programs for prevention. It also maintains a special hotline for referrals to local community services.

National Center on Child Abuse and Neglect (NCCAN) 404/546-0798
U.S. Children's Bureau/Office of Child
Development, DHHS, Washington DC 20013

A clearinghouse for information on child abuse and legal procedures in child abuse cases. Maintains regional offices throughout the country for reporting cases and gaining legal assistance.

Parents United   408/280-5055
PO Box 982, San Jose, CA 95108

Coordinates programs nationwide that deal with child incest and molestation. It has a hotline for referrals and crisis advice.

FOR LEGAL ASSISTANCE

Legal Advocates for Women (LAW)   415/752-9404
320 Clement St., San Francisco, CA 94118

Monitors legal cases involving women and provides educational materials on women's issues. Referrals for legal advice and assistance are also available.

National Clearinghouse on
Battered Women's Self-Defense
215/724-3270
910 South 49th St., Philadelphia, PA 19143

Provides assistance and support to battered women who have assaulted or killed their abusers while attempting to protect themselves. The project helps individuals and their advocates develop appropriate defense strategies for court.

National Victim Advocacy Center (NVADC)
817/877-3355
307 W. 7th St., Suite 1001, Ft. Worth, TX 76102

Provides resources for victim advocates and legal resources for attorneys handling victim suits against criminals or third parties.

National Organization for Victim Assistance (NOVA)
202/393-6682
717 D St. NW, Washington, DC 20004

A national organization with technical assistance to local victims assistance programs and referrals for victims nationally. It has a committee that specializes in domestic violence cases.

National Legal Aid Association (NLAA)
202/452-0620
1625 K St., NW, 8th Fl., Washington, DC 20006

Coordinates Legal Aid offices around the country which make legal assistance available to those who cannot afford it. Referral and eligibility information is also offered.

FOR ALCOHOL AND DRUG ABUSE

Al-Anon Family Group Headquarters (AL-ANON)
212/303-7240
PO Box 182, Grand Central
Station, New York, NY 10163

Coordinates self-help programs around the country for those with alcoholic spouses. Call to find out the closest Al-Anon group in your area.

110

Alcoholics Anonymous World Services (AA)
212/686-1100
Box 459, Grand Central Station,
New York, NY 10163

Center for A.A. programs nationwide, the self-help group for those who abuse alcohol. Supplies materials for potential A.A. members as well as listings of A.A. groups in your area.

Narcotics Anonymous World Service Office (NA)
818/780-3951
PO Box 999, Van Nuys, CA 91409

Like A.A. does for alcohol abusers, N.A. coordinates self-help programs for those addicted to drugs. You can contact them for the address and phone number of the N.A. meeting closest to you.

Human Services Institute (HSI)
813/746-7088
512-33rd Street Ct. West, Bradenton, FL 34205

Publishes and distributes a variety of books, workbooks, audio and video tapes on recovery from alcohol and drug addiction, on growing up in an alcoholic home, on eating disorders, and domestic violence. HSI features the *National Women's Directory of Alcohol and Drug Abuse Treatment and Prevention Programs*, which has a listing of nearly 1,000 programs for women nationwide.

111

INTRODUCTION

Several national hotlines offer immediate crisis counseling and referral to callers. Most are toll-free and available 24-hours-a-day. They can direct you or a violent man to the nearest program that should best meet your needs, as well as give you some good advice for the moment.

The best place to start is with a local battered women's shelter. Most shelters provide a crisis counseling hotline, a place to stay, and support groups for women not residing in the shelter. A shelter staff can probably best assess your situation and offer options for you to consider.

So call and talk to someone. There are many people eager to help and who know how to do it. Also consider urging a batterer to call any of these hotlines. Even though he may resist at first or not respond to the hotline advice, it could start him thinking about seeking help.

BATTERED WOMEN: 800/333-SAFE (NCADV)

Provides crisis counseling and referral to local shelters and women's centers. Its the first place to call if you're experiencing violence in the home and are unsure about the availability of a local shelter or shelter hotline.

BATTERERS: 617/547-9870
(Ending Men's Violence)

Offers referral to local programs for batters, more information about violent men, and crisis counseling for men.

CHILD ABUSE: 800/422-4453 (NCCAN)
800/222-2000 (NCCAF)

The numbers to call to report child abuse and get advice on the steps to take in child abuse cases. These hotlines also make referrals to local community services dealing with child abuse treatment and prevention.

CHILD MOLESTATION: 408/279-1957
(Parents United)

Provides information on what to do in cases of child molestation or incest. Also, makes referrals to local programs for molesters and their families.

ALCOHOL ABUSE: 800/448-8888

Immediate crisis counseling for alcohol abusers or those living with alcoholic partners. Offers referrals to local treatment programs and self-help groups.

114

DRUG ABUSE: 800/821-4357

Offers immediate crisis counseling to those abusing drugs or living with drug dependent partners. Also offers referrals to local treatment programs and self-help groups.

Note: Many additional books, articles, manuals, organizations, and films are listed in *Research on Men Who Batter: An Overview, Bibliography, and Resource Guide*, by Edward W. Gondolf (Bradenton, FL: Human Services Institute, 1988).

Annotated Bibliography

Domestic violence is no longer a deep secret. Over the past ten years countless books and articles have been written about domestic violence and how to stop it. Listed below is a selection of self-help and informational books on the subject. They are books written especially for battered women and for those who help them. The brief descriptions are intended as a guide to the books that might be most appropriate for your situation.

It is important to note that while more information on domestic violence may be useful, it is not a substitute for getting help from experienced program staff. Reading such books should supplement professional help. It should be one of many steps toward making a better life for yourself and your children.

FOR WOMEN

Getting Free: A Handbook for Women in Abusive Relationships, by Ginny NiCarthy (Seattle, WA: Seal Press, 1986).

This book remains the most popular guide for battered women. It explains the nature of abuse, its consequences, and how to get out of an abusive situation. The book also discusses how to deal with the confusion and emotional stress of an abusive relationship.

You Are Not Alone: A Guide for Battered Women, by Linda Rouse (Holmes Beach, FL: Learning Publications, 1984).

This widely-used guidebook is available both as a book and as an abridged booklet. It presents clearly and concisely the nature of physical and emotional abuse, an explanation of "the battering society," a profile and cautions about the battering man, and options for breaking the cycle of violence. The book concludes with sound advice for "taking care of oneself."

Men Who Hate Women and The Women Who Love Them: When Loving Hurts and You Don't Know Why, by Susan Forward and Joan Torres (New York: Bantam Books, 1986).

This acclaimed best-seller confronts the problem of emotionally abusive men — men who control, degrade, and use women. It notes the different kinds and consequences of non-physical abuse by men. The second half of the book is devoted to helping women deal with the abuse. It discusses how to set limits, maintain self-esteem, get professional help, and end the relationship.

Ending the Violence: A Guidebook Based on the Experiences of One Thousand Battered Wives, by Lee Bowker (Holmes Beach, FL: Learning Publications, 1986).

This book offers recommendations drawn from a study of women who managed to "beat wife beating." It summarizes formerly battered women's opinions of the clergy, police, and lawyers. Women shelters are considered the most effective in helping end the violence. It concludes with recommendations on "what works best" according to battered women who stopped the violence in their lives.

The Ones Who Got Away: Women Who Left Abusive Partners, by Ginny NiCarthy (Seattle, WA: Seal Press, 1987).

The stories of several battered women are recounted in this inspiring book. The stories offer examples of 35 women who found the courage and support to leave their violent partners and make a better life for themselves and their children.

Called to Account: The Story of One Family's Struggle to Say No to Abuse, by M'Liss Switzer and Katherine Hale (Seattle, WA: Seal Press, 1987).

This short book tells of one couple's effort to stop the violence and stay together. The role of the police and courts in getting the man to change his behavior are highlighted. The book presents a hopeful example of a responsive husband.

118

Shattered Dreams: The Story of Charlotte Fedders, by Charlotte Fedders and Laura Elliot (New York: Harper and Row, 1987).

Violence knows no class boundaries as the much publicized case of Charlotte Fedders demonstrates. This book tells of the years of abuse suffered by the wife of a public official in the Reagan administration. Fedders' efforts to finally leave her husband while risking adverse publicity are a highlight.

FOR MEN

Man to Man: A Guide for Men in Abusive Relationships, by Edward W. Gondolf and David Russell (Bradenton, FL: Human Services Institute, 1987).

This sixty-page guidebook is designed to confront men's excuses about their violence and prompt them to seek help. How to select a counseling program and steps toward establishing safety are discussed. Each chapter is introduced with stories of violent men and a resource section presents names of men's programs from around the country. This book should be the first a violent man receives.

Relapse: A Guide to Successful Recovery, by Dennis C. Daley (Bradenton, FL: Human Services Institute, 1987).

This booklet outlines the steps necessary to stop the drinking which so often accompanies violence, and ways to prevent relapse. The negative feelings and thinking associated with alcohol abuse are confronted along with the social pressures and cravings of drinking. Offers a concise and straight-forward place to start on the road to recovery from alcohol abuse.

Learning to Live Without Violence, by Dan Sonkin and Michael Murphy (San Francisco: Volcano Press, 1981).

This is a workbook for batterers designed to help them understand the nature of abuse and develop the skills to stop the violence. Each lesson includes exercises and questions to deal with topics like expressing emotions, dealing with anger, reducing stress, and communicating assertively. A section also deals with alcohol abuse and its role in intensifying violence.

119

This workbook is designed to be completed in conjunction with counseling and is not a substitute for seeking help.

Human Be-ing: How to Have a Creative Relationship Instead of a Power Struggle, by William Pietsch (New York, Signet, 1986).

The power struggle behind most abusive relationships is creatively addressed in this self-help book of words and drawings. It exposes the expectations brought from our childhood that cause conflict. It shows how to deal with one's real feelings and truly listen to those of another person. Practical steps to discovering and being oneself are also presented. The book concludes with the risks of change that often act as barriers and how to negotiate them. It is probably best suited for those men who have already begun attending a counseling program.

Touchstones: A Book of Daily Meditations for Men, by Hazelden Foundation (New York: Harper/Hazelden, 1987).

The book is a useful tool in confronting the overbearing expectations of the male sex role and the alcohol abuse and domestic violence that so often accompanies it. This pocket-size book contains a one-page inspirational reading for each day of the year. Each reading is introduced by a quotation from a range of well-known men, from famous sports figures to scientists like Einstein. The book is best suited for men who are in the process of change and are seeking some support to help them maintain it.

The Secrets Men Keep: Breaking the Silence Barrier, by Ken Druck (Garden City, NY: Doubleday, 1985).

A guide to improving men's emotional lives and developing a healthier sense of masculinity. Each chapter presents main points with examples from men's lives, and concludes with exercises for the reader to complete. The topics include dealing with hidden fears and doubts, the influence of our fathers, relations with male friends, improving one's sense of work, and responding to our spouses as partners and not as our "mother." This book is best suited for men in the process of change who are attempting to add maturity to their cessation of violence.

120

Let Go and Grow: Recovery for Adult Children, by Robert J. Ackerman (Pompano Beach, FL: Health Communications, 1987).

This motivating book identifies the characteristics of all adult children of alcoholics, plus the varying and diverse types of ACOA's. It identifies their positive characteristics and strengths as well as the problem areas, on which one bases a process of forgiving the past and changing the present. The insights are based on a study of 1,000 ACOA's as well as the author's experience as the nation's foremost expert in this field.

ABOUT BATTERED WOMEN

The Battered Woman, by Lenore Walker (New York: Harper and Row, 1979).

This is still the most widely-read book about battered women. Using accounts of battered women, the author discusses the myths of woman battering, the sense of learned helplessness that many battered women experience, and identifies the cycle of violence that often misleads women about the prospects for change.

The Family Secret: Domestic Violence in America, by William Stacey and Anson Shupe (Boston: Beacon Press, 1983).

A readable overview of the problems and options faced by battered women. It includes a chapter on children of violent families and concludes with a discussion of the alternatives battered women have when seeking safety. The book is based on surveys with Dallas shelter women. Its viewpoint is that our violent society is at fault.

Rape in Marriage, by Diane Russell (New York: Macmillian, 1982).

A thought-provoking account of the sexual abuse experienced by women in marriage based on interviews with over 200 women. It discusses the extent of marital rape, the kinds of rape, and reasons for this widespread abuse. Not only is marital

121

rape more prevalent than stranger rape, but it is also experienced in some form by over 40% of battered women.

When Battered Women Kill, by Angela Browne (New York: Free Press, 1987).

A powerful summation of 42 cases where battered women resorted to murder in self-defense. The book not only seeks to explain why some battered women resort to such extremes, but also shows why some women become desperately trapped in violent relationships. Many issues about the police and the court's response to domestic violence are raised.

Women and Male Violence: The Visions and Struggles of the Battered Women's Movement, by Susan Schechter (Boston: South End Press, 1982).

A feminist overview of the movement to establish shelters for battered women. It pointedly confronts the resistance to shelters as well as the internal growing pains that have confronted the growth of shelters. It strongly advocates organizing women to sustain the accomplishments and change society.

Violence Against Wives: A Case Against Patriarchy, by R. Emerson Dobash and Russell Dobash (New York: Free Press, 1979).

This ground-breaking book puts woman battering in its social and historical context and shows the battering to be an extension of men's power over women in society. It argues that violence against women be unequivocally condemned, the authority of husbands over wives be rejected, and the power relationships between men and women be changed.

Battered Women as Survivors: An Alternative to Treating Learned Helplessness, by Edward W. Gondolf with Ellen R. Fisher (Lexington, MA: Lexington Books/D.C. Heath, 1988).

The authors present a study of over 6,000 women from Texas shelters which counters the popular notion of learned helplessness, that women give up and give in to their abuse. It shows how women persistently seek different kinds of help despite the odds. It argues that psychological counseling and moral support are insufficient to meet the needs of battered women. A variety of resources and support services must be made available in order to more effectively assist battered women.

ABOUT VIOLENT MEN

Men Who Batter: An Integrated Approach to Stopping Wife Abuse, by Edward W. Gondolf (Holmes Beach, FL: Learning Publications, 1985).

This book presents a comprehensive discussion of why men batter, the kinds of treatment that are available to them, and a model of supervised self-help that can make a difference in batterers' lives. Its approach combines psychological and social explanations for abuse and notably argues for a long-term commitment to change that goes beyond anger control and towards confronting the male attitudes in a society that sustains battering of women.

Men Who Rape: What They Have to Say About Sexual Violence, by Thomas Benke (New York: St. Martin's, 1982).

In a series of provocative interviews with men from every walk of life, the author provides insight into the psyche of the American man. The book exposes how men view the rape of partners, friends or strangers as primarily an act of control and subjugation of women, rather than out of lust or passion. Responses from police, lawyers, and rape counselors are also included.

The Male Machine, by Mark Fasteau (New York: McGraw Hill, 1976).

This ground-breaking book still stands as one of the best descriptions of the male sex role. It vividly tells how men are socialized through sports, work, and the military into accepting violence as a means of getting their way. It considers the impact of this socialization on both the private and public side of

123

men's lives, from intimate relationships to foreign policy. It concludes with ideas about how we might raise men to be non-violent and less hateful toward women.

A Choice of Heroes: The Changing Faces of Manhood, by Mark Gerzon (New York: Houghton Mifflin, 1982).

This book presents a clear overview of where men have come from and where they should be headed. In the author's personal and historical account of manhood, he identifies the outmoded male images that dominate the outlook of most men: the frontiersman, soldier, breadwinner, expert, and lord. A new range of possibilities for men concludes the book and offers alternatives of what it means to "be a man."

Why Can't Men Open Up, by Steven Naifeh and Gregory White Smith (New York: Warner Books, 1984).

This book frankly exposes the hang-ups of men that lead many to close up. It discusses how the male culture works against intimacy by fostering a fear of dependency. It also offers suggestions on how to better communicate with men and help them overcome their ungrounded fears. Most appropriate for relationships where "the silent treatment" is a primary part of the psychological abuse.

How Men Feel: Their Response to Women's Demands for Equality and Power, by Allan Astrachan (Garden City, NY: Anchor/Doubleday, 1986).

This book reviews the response of men to the changes brought by the women's movement. Based on interviews with men across the country, it documents men's feelings about women in the workplace, women's new expectations about sexuality, and fathering. It shows that underlying much of the hostility and confusion between the sexes is men's continuing denial of women's competence and achievement. The book concludes with a discussion of the men's movement which is encouraging changes in men that benefit both men and women.

The Hearts of Men: American Dreams and the Flight from Commitment, by Barbara Ehrenreich (New York: Doubleday, 1983).

In this look at the recent developments of the male sex role, the author traces how cultural forces as diverse as Playboy magazine and the medical profession have caused the male flight from commitment. It shows that the so-called breakdown of the family was underway long before the women's movement began. Men who have shirked their family responsibilities for "the good life" have also been behind much of the backlash against the women's movement and the freedoms it has demanded for women.

Why Men Are the Way They Are, by Warren Farrell (New York: McGraw-Hill, 1986).

This book is based on the author's workshops on male-female relationships. It frankly discusses the powerlessness many men claim they experience and the problems this causes in relationships. Such questions as "Why are men so preoccupied with sex and success?" and "Why are men so afraid of commitment?" are addressed. Even though the book offers too much pity and justification for men, it may be useful to women considering new relationships.

Other books on domestic violence by the author:

Battered Women as Survivors: An Alternative to Treating Learned Helplessness, with Ellen Fisher (Lexington Books, 1988).

Research on Men Who Batter: An Overview, Bibliography, and Resource Guide (Human Services Institute, 1988).

Man to Man: A Guide for Men in Abusive Relationships, with David Russell (Human Services Institute, 1987).

Men Who Batter: An Integrated Approach to Stopping Wife Abuse (Learning Publications, 1985).